Clear Your Shit

A Bible for Accelerated Evolution

By Dane Tomas

First published in 2015 by Dane Tomas Enterprises

© Dane Tomas
The moral rights of the author have been asserted.

National Library of Australia Cataloguing-in-Publication data:

Author:
> Tomas, Dane

Title:
> Clear Your Shit: A Bible For Accelerated Evolution/ Dane
> Tomas

ISBN 13:
> 978-1519302861

ISBN 10:
> 151930286X

Subjects:
> Consciousness
> Spirituality
> Emotional healing (Psychology)
> Self-Actualization (Psychology)

This book is dedicated to the unseen, underlying field of consciousness that permeates all things and compels us to expand and evolve endlessly and forever.

Table of Contents

Before enlightenment, chopping wood, carrying water.
After enlightenment, chopping wood, carrying water.
                                    - Zen proverb

PART ONE:

ORIGINS &
INTENTIONS

I've been asked many times why the work I do leads to such deep, fast, intense and permanent transformation. Often the people asking this question are very spiritually and emotionally developed individuals who've done decades of deep self-work and personal exploration. Often they are teachers and practitioners in their own right.

Yet still, we clear one 'little thing' and their whole reality changes in a way they've never experienced before. After the changes take place and they recompose themselves, there's one question they want to ask:

"How is that possible?"

My answer to this question is the same for them as it is for my students, and for everyone who's started learning the magical-seeming tool we call 'Self-Clearing'.

The power of transformative work is really only limited by the following factors:

The level of consciousness, and strength of intention of the practitioner.

It seems fitting then that I should set a clear and powerful intention for this book before going any further.

I'm writing this so that anyone who is looking for a way to set themselves free of their unconscious and limiting behavior can do so for themselves, without needing the help of a practitioner, coach, mentor or 'guru'.

I'm also writing for those who wish to keep growing and expanding, far beyond their humble beginnings, and for those who want to experience deep fulfillment and live a life in which their gifts to the world are given fully.

If you adopt the frameworks and concepts outlined in this book, and practice the simple tool I demonstrate in the free video training that accompanies this book there is quite literally no limit to what you can experience.

I created this technology because I don't think it's fair that our earliest circumstances shape our beliefs about what is possible. I believe that we can Be, Do and Have WHAT-EVER we truly desire IF we're prepared to let go of what holds us back.

I've had the opportunity to observe over a thousand people engage with this work at one level or another. These range from those random drop-ins who visited me when I ran a small Kinesiology clinic to the die-hards who've attended every program and workshop I've ever delivered. I'm particularly lucky to have been able to learn from those who've taken these tools and made them part of their daily lives.

Clearing is used in a million different ways. For me it's a tool for my spiritual evolution as well as for helping me accelerate my practical skills (there's no way I could've written this book without it!). I've watched entrepreneurs use it to double and triple their incomes, lovers use it to become more orgasmic and I've watched others use it to finally leave behind the scars and trauma caused by loss and abuse.

Regardless of your particular focus for improvement and healing, learning the frameworks in this book and practicing the practical tool of self-clearing is like having an upgraded mental and emotional operating system.

This book is the first attempt at an official handbook for this work. It's here to explain the philosophy behind it, to break down some of the key ideas that make it fit together and also to give clear instructions on how to do the different types of clears that I've come up with over the last fifteen years.

For those new to the whole thing it will serve as an introduction and provide some context to something you may have seen or heard about but don't really understand yet.

For those who are a lot deeper down the rabbit hole (my clearing super nerds) this book is very much for you too. It's here to clarify some of the questions you've asked me and to function as a reference book for you and your family, friends and clients.

Because this book is designed to accompany a practical skill, it's highly recommended you sign up for the free self-clearing video training at:

www.clearyourshit.com

You can also subscribe to the 'Clear Your Shit' YouTube channel which houses many hours of instructional videos, talks and additional learning resources.

How This all Came About

The more clearing and other forms of spiritual work I've done the more accessible the memories of my early childhood have become. I have a direct sense of what it was like when I was born, and in my first few years, and the general feeling I get is that I didn't really like what I experienced when I found myself in a body and on planet earth.

I was raised by loving parents: a strong, practical father and a loving mother who has the unusual position of being as equally versed in western medical science as in holistic and complimentary medicine and energy work.

This definitely had a strong impact on what I have perceived as 'normal'; I have naturally gravitated towards the mystical, the magical and the unseen from a very young age.

This has gone through all the "typical" stages of reading runes and tarot as a child, to studying shamanism and ritual magic as a teen and then into psychology, personal development, Taoism, Buddhism, Jungian psychology and ultimately with me undertaking a comparative religion degree at the University of Queensland in my early twenties.

Needless to say, this has given me some broad frameworks with which to view the world and in my late twenties I began to see clearly which ideas and modalities resonated with me most strongly.

For the last fifteen or so years I have experimented relentlessly with personal development, NLP, Buddhism, Traditional Chinese Medicine (TCM), Tantra, the work of Carl Jung, the work of John Demartini and as a functional way to bring it all together – Kinesiology.

By 2012 I was running a small coaching business and beginning to incorporate some of the tools and practices I'd been using in my own life for over a decade into my work.

Rather than just ask people questions and help them mentally navigate their way past obstacles I wanted to reach inside and remove the blockages and incongruence that I could sense beneath the surface.

I'd been using Kinesiology informally and very experimentally since 2000 but the day I started using it with my clients everything began to accelerate.

The coaching industry provides coaches with great maps and models of human behavior but their ability to know what's beneath the surface for a client is based solely on intuition and 'sensory acuity' which can take thousands of hours to develop.

The kinesiologists have direct in-roads to be able to talk to the body and unconscious mind directly. As practitioners in general, they are amazingly in tune with emotions and the modality tends to attract caring, deeply feeling individuals.

If there's a downside to the modality, it's that most kinesiologists don't have well-developed maps and models of how human behavior works. It's a very gentle and nurturing sort of an art, practitioners often have a very soft approach that can take a long time to get to the bottom of emotional issues.

What I recognized early on was that combining the coaching language and mental maps with the kinesiologist's ability to talk directly to the body would create something completely new and very powerful.

I've always been fascinated by the phenomenon of consciousness, and for years have been looking for the really effective maps of consciousness.

How are we and how is reality structured?

By January 2013 my house was starting to look like a mad scientist's workshop.

There were diagrams and charts strewn everywhere, with sections crossed out and arrows connecting one model to another. Something was coming together, but I couldn't see the full implication of what it was yet.

Right in the center of my table lay the three diagrams I was most fascinated by:

1. A traditional diagram of the seven chakras
2. An info graphic of the Spiral Dynamics spiral
3. A chart depicting Dr David Hawkins' infamous 'Scale of Consciousness'

These pictures sat on my table for days. There had been other models I'd attempted to integrate but they just weren't as fundamental to what I was trying to understand as these three.

These three pieces of paper are what I consider the most powerful and accurate maps for understanding consciousness and human evolution.

What I loved (and am blown away by to this day) is that these understandings have come from very different sources, yet from my perspective they all seem to be communicating the same thing.

They each imply that reality is vibrational and certain resonances and behaviors occur at each different level of vibration. They even agree pretty closely on WHICH behaviors and resonances turn up at each level.

I sat there staring at them, unsure if I was going mad or if I had stumbled onto something really important.

I muscle-tested various questions and possibilities and tested the vibrational levels of the individual models and the vibrational levels of the models combined.

The overall combination of the models tested up at 1000 (which is the top of the scale of consciousness) and gradually I began playing with them to create a sort of integrated super map of consciousness which would go on to inform EVERYTHING I built from this point onwards.

Interestingly it had only been months since I'd discovered and integrated the skill of self-muscle-testing. After twelve years of having to bully my girlfriend, flatmate or unsuspecting student kinesiologists into being my muscle-testing dummies, I could finally accurately measure ANYTHING that was going on in my own body, whether physically, emotionally, energetically, mentally or spiritually.

It also meant I was free to conduct experiments with my own consciousness 24/7. I began thinking about the three maps a LOT and started conducting research on my own energetic field.

The first thing I started to ask myself (whilst staring at Hawkins' scale) was "Can I change my level of consciousness just by clearing up my emotional blocks?"

The answer was a resounding YES.

So, although Hawkins suggests that a 'normal' human might evolve only a few points on his scale of consciousness in a whole lifetime, I was starting to see that as a very unambitious way of looking at things.

After all, if our emotions are simply energies vibrating at certain frequencies and consciousness is a frequency also, dropping out the low-vibrational emotions would surely raise our vibration?

I decided to put my new theory to the test.

I muscle-tested my current level of consciousness; it was 400.

Not bad, but for a guy who'd done a lifetime of spiritual and emotional work, not really that encouraging.

According to the scale, 400 is the vibrational level of rational thought, logic and thinking.

I then tested "Are there any patterns or emotions right now that prevent me from being at 1000?"

The answer again was a strong yes. I started doing some clearing. Lots of shame and dogma tested up.

Religious and social programming tells us we're unworthy, and we're separate from God and we're "not the messiah, just a very naughty boy!"

That's how these patterns seemed, like layers of traditional rules and programs that prevent an individuals from feeling our divinity.

Once the heavy emotions began to shift I could feel myself expanding and opening. I felt myself shifting energetically and was slightly dizzy; it was almost like getting stoned but I felt myself getting CLEARER rather than duller.

Then I felt awash with peacefulness and a sort of wide-awake bliss.

When I muscle-tested the new level of consciousness, I was now resonating at 600.

Wow. I just jumped 200 points from a couple of clears. This began to confirm a theory I've held for years.

IT IS OUR CONDITIONING THAT SEPARATES US FROM UNIVERSAL CONSCIOUSNESS.

Babies have always looked like little Buddhas to me.

Energetically clean and clear. Open. Expressive. Present. Radiant.

Then we gradually load them up with programs and patterns and the cultural weight of fear and expectation and conditional love until they're just as energetically dirty as the rest of us!

If it were possible for a child to grow up and learn without taking on the energetic weight of his or her parents, they would remain just as shiny and innocent and pure as a newborn baby.

We can see this energy in the so-called gurus of the world. All that has happened is through one process or experience or another these people have become energetically 'cracked open' and their inner light is able to shine though.

I decided to push my luck with the clearing, even though a deep sense of foreboding about cracking into 'ascended master territory' was starting to arise.

I cleared ALL the blocks between me and 1000.

It was like taking an elevator up to God. Except once I'd knocked out the resistance between myself and the part on the scale labelled as enlightenment I felt ... nothing. Like, literally nothing.

I could feel my consciousness expanding out through the walls of my crappy apartment and a deep expanse of nothingness.

It was weird but I liked it. I felt, for the first time ever in my life, that I was completely clear.

I started clearing myself 'up to 1000' every day. I was able to see the world from a non-attached place. Good events and bad events in my life began to just seem like events.

Death became less scary and there was a sense of okay-ness that permeated absolutely everything.

It wasn't that emotions didn't exist anymore. They still arose as they always had; I could be just as angry as before. The difference was that I felt as if the 'real me' was sitting in the background watching it all play out.

Even if I was in a bad mood I could feel a sense of space and even humor around it.

I could sense that my consciousness had opened right up.

I could also feel that I wasn't necessarily radiating more love or more power or that I wasn't any more mentally intelligent or experiencing any of the things I might have associated with 'enlightenment' or 'awakening'.

I just WAS.

From this point onwards the clearing technology, my reputation and my business started developing REALLY fast.

I had been playing with a process that was a cross between Kinesiology and NLP timeline.

This eventually became known as a 'root clear'.

This clear would become the building block of the Spiral and also became one of the things that made the work I teach so much more powerful than old-school Kinesiology.

The ROOT CLEAR is about going right to the roots of an emotional block. It changes our entire relationship to the thing we're clearing.

As I've been famously quoted as saying (to the horror of many kinesiologists), "Why would we want to peel the layers of the onion? I'm going to just explode the fucking onion."

In a normal Kinesiology session an emotion like fear might come up — the body will be rebalanced and reset and the person will let go of THAT specific fear.

But what about targeting the healing at the person's RELA-TIONSHIP to fear itself?

What if we could release the emotions that caused the person to contract unnecessarily in the face of fear?

That wouldn't mean that the person would never feel fear but that the person would become okay with feeling fear. They would feel it and be able to expand through it and not run any of the associated patterns that cause them to shut down when facing an uncertain outcome.

Basically this process would rapidly accelerate what the most practical spiritual practices teach us to do very gradually.

To BE present to whatever is going on and to open through it whilst not REACTING to it.

I started ROOT CLEARING anything and everything to see what would happen.

Undeniably root clears were exponentially stronger than the simple concept or statement clears I'd being doing for years. I'd soon learn this wasn't always a good thing!

Most notably I started root clearing Shame and Guilt (the two emotions that sit right at the bottom of the scale of consciousness) for people with the expectation that it would increase their sense of self-worth and help with wealth building.

I did this on about fifty clients throughout 2012 and 2013.

The results were groundbreaking. Some of them quit their jobs immediately, some attracted new partners and many started to make a lot more money almost overnight. A few also had diarrhea for five days after clearing two of the heaviest emotions known to man. (These emotions just happen to be associated with the large intestine meridian in Chinese medicine!)

Why did these big changes happen?

Shame and guilt both negate WORTH. They are not 'primal' emotions like sadness or anger or fear but are in fact man-made, toxic emotions. Shame dates back to our tribal ancestry when being kicked out of the group meant total disconnection and most likely death.

Guilt evolved a little later as organized religion and nation states and laws evolved. It's typically a response to not living up to an external injected set of values and rules. Both of these emotions have been fundamental to the survival of our species. The presence of shame and guilt in people ensures we band together, stick to the plan and follow the rules. These emotions also make it hard to connect strongly with your own desire or think independently.

As these energies drop away we start to automatically regard ourselves as being WORTHY. We are able to connect to our natural abundance and our ability to feel deserving, connected and to express ourselves begins to increase. Without the tendency to second guess our decisions and beat ourselves up we also get much more effective at acting on our desires.

Interestingly our moral compass and conscience still functions perfectly without carrying strong residual shame or guilt. So far no-one has experienced an increase in illegal activity after going through these clears!

As our self-worth develops we begin to establish a clearer relationship with our OWN values and morality which allows us to value other people as well as ourselves and to trust in our own ability to do what's right.

After witnessing the effects of the Shame and Guilt clearing on people, I realized I was onto something and went back to my maps.

What would be the best clears to accelerate human evolution?

Which emotions MOST prevented us from climbing the Spiral Dynamics ladder, opening all seven chakras and vibrating at the top of the scale of consciousness?

After a lot of experimentation, testing, measuring and tweaking I arrived at a chart with seven sections (one corresponding to each level of Spiral Dynamics and to each of the seven chakras) and assigned three key emotions to each level.

Playing with these maps and muscle-testing the vibrational measure of hundreds of different combinations soon became a trance-like, creative channeling process.

I allowed the maps and models to come through me and used my natural ability to recognize complex patterns and FEEL energetically what lined up.

What came together was a mixture of logic and intuition. I was able to see something that I don't think anyone else had yet recognized but that was ALREADY THERE waiting to be found.

Another thing that felt weird as hell was ... I used this system to build itself.

I was using self-testing and the scale of consciousness to measure each and every piece of the map I put together. If it didn't resonate at 1000 (absolute truth) then I would align it to something that did.

In this way I arrived at the map I would later use to clean up the baggage of everyone I knew. The most appropriate name I could think of was 'The Spiral'.

As the first person to go through this work it COMPLETE-LY turned my life upside down. I realize in hindsight that it took away a huge amount of the dysfunctional patterns that had largely defined me as a person and gave me full permission to be myself. It's taken some time to work out who that really is!

Initially I took my friends and business partners through and then after the first twenty-five people had all sur-vived I started taking people through in groups for a small fee.

The process has since been copied by other practitioners and even altered but ...

I don't think those people really understand what it IS, what it does and why this specific structure is what makes it so powerful.

There is something about the structure of a SPIRAL that is central to human nature (look at our DNA) and that perfectly describes the way we ascend and evolve.

Random clearing work will still raise your vibration and allow you to develop latent abilities but completing The Spiral process unlocks a dormant intelligence that perme-ates every aspect of your life.

After going through The Spiral my ability to see and feel my own patterns (as well as those of others) became much more precise. I started experimenting with Wealth Clearing and Manifestation Clearing and soon found myself running a half-a-million-dollar-a-year business.

Several hundred people went through The Spiral and all around me strange things were starting to happen. Poor hippies were turning entrepreneurial. Uptight business coaches were going to tantra workshops and having full body orgasms and I began to wonder if I'd unleashed the apocalypse.

It turns out I hadn't. And I learned a lot from seeing people using this work over time. I began training others in these methods, ranging from short one-day self-clearing workshops to weeklong intensive practitioner trainings.

What emerged over time was this awareness that something in us WANTS to evolve. I firmly believe that our consciousness knows what it's doing and is hungry to expand, accelerate, be free and carry us towards our full potential.

Two years after taking myself through The Spiral process I changed my name.

I realized that I personally created this work to dig myself out from the heavy Anglo-Saxon conditioning that had me feeling so limited as a teenager and I reached a point where (after fifteen years) I no longer needed to 'heal' anything.

I realized that if I wasn't 'complete' now, I never would be.

Since then I've used clearing in a different way. I don't use it to get away from pain and difficulty. I design the life I want to live, boldly step towards it and feel supported by the fact I KNOW I can handle any emotional resistance or sabotage that might arise in the process.

How to Use This Book

I recommend reading through this book once (it's not that long) and then using it as a reference. If you haven't yet signed up for the free self-clearing video training or attended a workshop, definitely do that. From there it's about finding YOUR way of using this tool.

The basic things I recommend are:

- Finding any critically limiting emotional wounds or traumas and clearing them
- Actively designing your life using the life master planning sheets
- Using clearing to clear any resistance to that vision
- Creating a daily morning ritual that involves clearing your chakras and energy field
- Getting the basic self-clearing skills (video) mastered
- Sharing your intentions in the Facebook 'Self-Clearing Study Circle' group

THE SELF-CLEARING
PHILOSOPHY

Before we get into the technical and practical aspects of clearing there is a philosophical framework that needs to be understood and embraced in order to get the full potency of this work.

There are a lot of coaches, kinesiologists, healers, energy workers and people who facilitate personal and spiritual growth in one way or another out there.

Many of them regularly create powerful healing spaces and positive change for other people, but struggle to use their skills to further their own growth and evolution.

The problem with that, firstly, is that these people ultimately are operating as a healer or a teacher driven by their own unresolved wounds.

Secondly, any practitioner or facilitator can only take you as far as they themselves are prepared to go. If a healer doesn't have the ability for courageous self-reflection and have tools to continue their own evolution, sooner or later you will outgrow them.

This is the aspect that makes a practitioner who embraces the following framework so powerful.

What's starting to happen now is that a culture of people who have the right mental maps and the ability to self reflect and take action on their insights is growing around the 'Clear Your Shit' banner.

Throughout the first ten years of the exploratory journey I've been on, I was seeking to answer one question above all others:

"If so much of my behavior and conditioning is taking place on an unconscious level – how can I locate the patterns that are REALLY running the show?"

Over time I've evolved a framework that's helped me do one of the most difficult things: look directly at myself, work out which unconscious aspects of me are influencing my life and then consciously engage with those aspects.

Alfred Korzybski (the father of general semantics) taught us "the map is not the territory". In other words, the symbolic constructs our mind makes up to help us navigate the world are not necessarily accurate representations of the outside world itself.

We can, however, use the mismatches BETWEEN the map and the territory to help us see ourselves in a more honest light.

If you're like me, you're probably thinking: "Let's just get to the bit where I learn how to DO the actual thing."

Here's the problem with that. Clearing our stuff without fully embracing the idea that the world is a mirror doesn't really work that well.

Plenty of people learn a bit of this stuff and then walk around saying things like:

"My husband is annoying; can I clear that?"
"I don't make any money; can I clear that?"
"My knee hurts; can I clear that?"

All of these things are external events, meaning they are SYMPTOMS rather than causes. The real causes of these kinds of problems – are internal.

I might have a conversation with the woman being triggered by her husband and end up having her clear a statement like: "I'm okay with being judgmental" or "I'm okay with receiving support" or something else that on the surface seems like it has nothing to do with her husband "being annoying".

Every situation reveals deep truths about us, if we're prepared to look.

I've combined this overall philosophy into something I call 'Mirror Theory'.

Let's take a look at what that entails.

The Assumptions of Mirror Theory

Mirror Theory is the art of using the outside world to show you your hidden self. It can be held together by adopting the following principles AS IF they were true.

I am responsible:

What Stephen Covey calls 'proactivity' means understanding that at any given moment there are some things that we can control and other things that we can't.

In order to be empowered it's important to be able to:
a)   tell these two things apart and
b)   learn to focus on the things we can control, also known as our 'sphere of influence'

We cannot control the actions of others, disasters that take place outside our influence or things that have already happened. We can't necessarily even control the emotions that come up for us once they've come up but we can choose:

1.   What we focus on
2.   What we tell ourselves about what happens
3.   How we engage with the emotion that arises
4.   What we do next

This framework doesn't imply that you are in charge of everything, that you magically control all events or that you are to blame for large-scale global events.

It simply means that we are ABLE to RESPOND to our experience. Even in a typically disempowering situation (for example, being thrown in jail) we get to choose what lessons we draw from the situation, what meanings we derive from it, how we manage and process the emotions that arise inside our body and what actions we take within the sphere of influence we do have.

Many people seem to find this principle offensive, especially those who are emotionally invested in the view that the world is a hostile and unfair place.

I use this framework not as an absolute truth, but as a filter to help me moderate the fact that my mind has been drastically shaped by the narratives of my past experiences.

The interesting thing about the self-responsibility frame is that those who adopt it (even if it may seem untrue at first) become more proactive, more influential and more empowered.

This becomes much easier to live by when we have a tool like self-clearing up our sleeve because we realize that emotionally charged perceptions and painful triggers can be dropped in an instant IF we have the courage to take ownership of our own experience.

Perception is projection:

One of the biggest influences drawn from Carl Jung and later from NLP is the idea that everything we perceive is on some level influenced by our unconscious mind and our mental filters. Once we take this into account it allows us to understand the subjective nature of our viewpoint and provides great insight into helping us understand what UNCONSCIOUS behaviors are playing out in our life.

My advice with this idea is to apply it ONLY to:

a) ourselves and
b) those people who have explicitly given us permission, right now, to reflect the patterns we see playing out in their lives

Don't become that person who walks around accusing everyone else of 'projecting' but refuses to look at their own illusions!

'Perception is projection' addresses the notion that we can NEVER get outside of our own heads. If we can perceive something, we are on some level creating it.

We see the world through our filters which include (but aren't limited to) our five senses, our beliefs, our values, our culture, our current emotional state, our memories and so on.

Literally ANYTHING we experience is simply a mirror of our internal environment. This doesn't mean it doesn't exist outside of us, simply that we will never experience an unfiltered, unbiased, unconditioned view of it.

We will never know 'the truth', only 'our truth'.

In fact, because our filters are SO strong we constantly filter the world (which is infinitely complex) and look for events and experiences that confirm what we already believe to be true. This is a large part of why we play out the same patterns over and over again. It's also a part of why clearing one simple emotion that holds an old belief in place can allow us to experience something we never thought possible (like effortless financial abundance or deep love and intimacy without fear or letting go of twenty years of grief in a single moment).

We live inside the world inside our head, not inside the world directly. Knowing this empowers us to realize that if we want to change the world, we must first change ourselves.

A simple rule of thumb is, if I can see a trait in someone else, I definitely possess that trait myself. Maybe they're expressing something I'm currently repressing. Maybe they're repressing something I'm currently expressing.

It's not always simple to deduce the EXACT pattern we're running immediately but if there's a feeling of discordance or 'trigger' when observing a person or an event then there's something we haven't yet owned or dealt with internally.

NOTE: This doesn't mean we allow others' dysfunctional behavior in our lives and it doesn't mean we shouldn't take action against injustice.

It DOES mean there's always something to learn AND if you have basic clearing skills up your sleeve, it's quite easy to own and integrate any trait you're projecting IF you have the courage to be honest with yourself.

Once we fully embrace the idea that our entire reality is made of our perceptions, which are themselves conditioned by past events and inner biases, we realize we CAN create absolute magic in our lives JUST by changing beliefs, emotional patterns, images we hold and stories we tell ourselves.

This principle also leads to deeper compassion for others since once we start realizing that EVERYONE is projecting their experience all the time, we stop expecting others to conform to our particular value system and perception.

How I do anything is how I do everything:

This is an extension of the other two principles and can help us really zero in on the specifics of the big patterns that run our lives.

Another way to say this is that our 'micro' patterns show us our 'macro' patterns.

I remember sweeping floors as a teenager and being really diligent about the first 80% of it and then as I got to the end, getting bored and disaffected and doing a half-assed job.

Someone told me this rule and I realized: I didn't just do that when sweeping floors, I was doing it in EVERY area of my life. Patterns you're running in your business will also be running in your relationships. We like to look at our life as though it's neatly segmented into categories but our unconscious mind doesn't work like that.

In fact, the unconscious mind LOVES to generalize. This is why traumatic events like death of loved ones, sexual or physical abuse, relationship break-ups, etc. can have such a HUGE influence on us across multiple areas.

In times of severe emotional pain we often make unconscious decisions not just about specifics but also about big, generalized concepts that will affect our whole life.

Let's say I'm working with someone who suffered sexual abuse in their childhood.

Although the specific issue and story we're dealing with is:

"I was abused"

Generic beliefs (supported by strong emotional anchors) are likely to be things like:

"Nobody respects my boundaries"
"I'm unworthy
"I'm dirty"
"I don't like receiving"
"People are untrustworthy"
"Sex is destructive"

There will usually be dozens of very generalized beliefs and ideas that we will form strong emotional charge around. A lot of these beliefs won't make any sense to us as adults, but then, they weren't formed by adults. These beliefs and emotional patterns will run our lives until the moment we recognize them and fully release them.

Carrying the belief that "I'm unworthy" won't just show up in our love life. It will affect our success with business and wealth building and prevent us from going after what we want in life. Restrict our ability to express our creativity and uniqueness, and turn up in dozens of other areas too.

We can be doing work twenty years later and suddenly realize how an event is affecting us in a way that make no logical sense.

"I just realized I've kept myself broke since my mother died!"

Once we start practicing this rule we can know a LOT about someone just from a small mannerism or a pattern that's repeated a couple of times in a short conversation. The real art once again is, can we turn this principle in on ourselves?

When we see a habit that is dysfunctional in one area of our life (like sweeping the floor), we can ask – where else does this pattern play out in my life?

When we bring these three ideas together we create a new mental operating framework that tells us:

- we are driving our own life
- we can learn and take ownership of any event and
- much of what we perceive to be true is made up

These ideas may or may not be true. That doesn't matter one bit. What does matter is that we adopt this framework to open up our range of options and support us in lovingly seeing ourselves for who we are.

In practicality this framework is much more useful when we have the ability to talk to our unconscious mind using muscle-testing and to let go of any block we want using clearing.

The key skill that needs to be developed is that of asking ourselves insightful questions that unpack the hidden drivers of our behavior. This is the part that can take a little while to get good at and like anything it takes practice.

Included in the final section of this book are some tools that can support you in developing that skill set.

You'll find both a list of useful questions for narrowing down what's really going on and for finding out HOW life is mirroring your inner emotional patterns.

On top of that there's also a self-coaching template that you can work your way through to find and overcome ANY emotional or mental hurdle.

This book and this work deals primarily with our inner world and the Mirror Theory framework is perfect for this area.

That doesn't deny the existence of the physically mea-surable outside world, or contradict the laws of physics or imply that everything that ever happened to anyone is 'because they manifested it'. Reality is much more complex than that and can't be explained in three little rules.

If you adopt this framework and it works for you please understand that NOTHING in this book is any sort of absolute truth. Don't become 'that guy' or 'that girl' who pushes their beliefs on their friends.

I have found that when people try to force these sorts of frameworks on others they lose potency. The ultimate intention here is to equip you with a belief system designed to help you see the aspects of yourself that are hidden in shadow, integrate them and move forwards in creating a spectacular life.

PART TWO:

THE TOOL

Although the bulk of this work and the power of this particular branch of healing is all in the conceptual frameworks and in the strength of our intention none of it would work at all without one simple little piece borrowed from Kinesiology.

In 1964 Dr George Goodheart discovered that muscle response could be used as a way of gathering information from the body. This discovery led to the creation of Applied Kinesiology which later led to the creation of other branches of Kinesiology such as PKP, Touch For Health, etc.

Self muscle-testing puts this process quite literally in our own hands.

For those of you who haven't yet seen the process I recommend going to the www.clearyourshit.com page right now and watching the introductory video before continuing with the rest of the book.

As you can see it's quite a simple process. We form a circle with our thumb and pinky finger and interlock that circle with another circle formed by the thumb and index finger on our other hand.

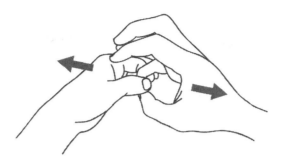

LOCKED

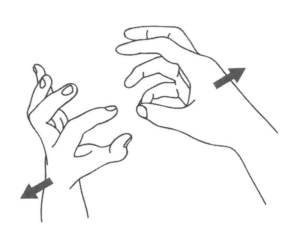

UNLOCKED

We then gently pull the two rings against each other, feeling how the closed circuits created by each finger and thumb naturally hold together.

Through repeated practice we anchor this feeling of 'locked' to a sense of 'YES'.

As we say "NO" we allow ourselves to feel the subtle weakening of the circuitry and notice that the fingers unlock.

At first it feels like we're 'making it happen' but as we practice it we gradually build a sense of certainty and can feel that the body is able to speak to us through this simple OFF/ON or YES/NO circuit.

Throughout this learning process remember that you're installing a new piece of software into your body and teaching your nervous system a simple way to communicate with you.

If it feels 'made up', don't worry; that's exactly how I felt when someone first showed me the finger-testing method.

After practicing for two weeks though, I began to notice that the results were getting more consistent.

After doing it for three months I no longer questioned if I was 'making it up' any more than I questioned whether Google search results were 'real'. I just put my enquiry into the system and I get answers!

Ultimately this process is about self-trust; if you practice it then you'll notice it starts to work.

And since trust is like a muscle, the best way to build it is walk around the house testing everything you can think of and seeing what happens!

Once we've practiced this for a little while we can start testing our congruence with verbal statements, with objects, with different types of food.

This muscle-testing ability is an enormous breakthrough. It means for the first time we can build a communication bridge between our unconscious mind and our conscious mind. We can ask ANYTHING we want, so long as we can phrase the question in a way that it has a yes/no or numerical answer.

This tool can then be applied to all the different models and processes in this book as well as to thousands of other applications.

The benefit of it is, you can find out if your unconscious mind (which runs about 85% of your life including all of your vital physical processes) is onboard with your conscious level intentions.

This mismatch is the cause of the vast bulk of our resistance and self-sabotage (not to mention a large percentage of our disease).

The long-term benefit of this tool is it allows you to experience greater alignment between your day-to-day life and who you really are!

What is Clearing?

In many ways the word 'clearing' is a bit deceptive.

It implies we can just hit delete on a belief or an emotional pattern and it disappears.

That's not exactly what happens.

We use this tool to let go of beliefs, emotions and energetic blocks that shape our behavior. They don't just disappear though; they have to be integrated, learned from and then moved past into a new way of being.

Depending on what sort of patterns we're clearing up this can happen instantly or take a few weeks to integrate fully.

Working out which actions to take to support the work we've done and help us move into a new behavioral reality is a secondary skill that has to be learned too.

Another take on the word 'clearing' is that we are clearing the obstacles from our life path.

When we focus this tool on a specific area of our life, such as our financial wealth, our career or business path, our sex life, our relationship or WHATEVER, we start to develop our skills and abilities in that area MUCH faster than the 'normal' speed at which a human being grows.

This is largely to do with the limiting effect that our conditioning has on our ability to learn and grow.

There are layers and layers of handed-down emotional and mental programming that date back all the way to our caveman ancestry.

We all have conditioning based on the environments our ancestors lived in and on the types of events our ancestors had to deal with. All of this conditioning is passed down from one generation to the next, much like genes are. In addition to this we accumulate new conditioning from the moment we're born and throughout the events we experience growing up.

Much of this conditioning seems pretty harmless, although there's no question in my view that the emotional patterns we carry affect our physical health and limit the functioning of our body as well as our mind.

The most immediately noticeable problems, though, occur when we try to head down a path we HAVEN'T been well conditioned for.

What happens when a person with deep ancestral patterns of scarcity (most of us) tries to become legitimately wealthy?

Or when an individual with generations of sexual repression decides to start exploring pleasure and erotic expression?

Dissonance or incongruence are ways of describing what happens when we consciously pursue something but our unconscious mind (which controls our body) starts to throw up resistance and self-sabotage patterns to stop us from doing something we unconsciously perceive as threatening.

This is usually what brings a person to me or to one of my practitioners. They are working as hard as they can to succeed in one or more areas of their life and they know that something they don't understand is holding them back.

This is where clearing (especially combined with some kind of coaching or mentoring program) is profoundly effective.

It's the equivalent of taking the handbrake off the car before setting off on a long journey.

The Clearing Process

The actual act of clearing a behavioral pattern or a complex (more on complexes later) follows this basic structure:

1. Identify the triggering event
2. Muscle-test through the emotions chart to find the exact emotion triggered
3. Map the structure of the emotion (optional)
4. Rub the corresponding emotional release points and breathe
5. Retest to see if the emotion has been cleared
6. Choose an activity to help integrate (optional)
7. Get on with your life

How to know which points to rub:

Work out which points to rub by looking up which points correspond to the meridian listed on the emotions chart OR you can just gently hold the ESR (Emotional Stress Relief) points in the diagram below.

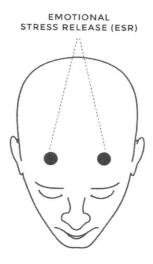

EMOTIONAL
STRESS RELEASE (ESR)

How to Use Numbers and Percentages Whilst Clearing

So far we've described using the muscle-test to obtain yes/ no or lock/unlock type answers. In fact, we can use a muscle-test to obtain any answer that can be communicated by an 'indicator change'.

Every time I file through a list, such as in the emotions chart, I'm simply looking for the 'odd one out'.

If I test through the stomach meridian list – empathy, sympathy, disgust, worry – and the muscle-test breaks on 'worry' then I know that 'worry' is the emotion I'm looking for because the response from the muscle-test has gone from a lock (for the first three emotions) to an unlock on the one that has a trigger attached to it.

Likewise, I can test through numbers in this way (you'll learn this when you do root clearing) – 1, 2, 3, 4 – and when the muscle unlocks on '5' I know that 5 is the number I'm looking for.

This can also be used with percentages which give a much greater accuracy when working through things like Manifestation Clears or when working in an area we know has a LOT of layers of emotions related to it.

If I'm clearing the emotions from my shoulder which I injured years ago and I know holds a lot of different emotions, I can measure as a percentage how clear it is: as I release one emotion after another it moves from 50%, 60%, 70%, etc. with 100% indicating that it's completely clear.

This gives accuracy to measurement and is commonly used when Brain Clearing, Body Clearing, Manifestation Clearing, Energy Field Clearing, etc.

Mapping Emotions

For those of us who want more details about the nature of the emotion there is a three-part framework we can test our way through to get much more specific information about WHAT the emotion relates to.

Let's say I've just been fired from my job. I might come up with a simple statement like:

"I'm okay with losing my job"

On testing I find out that the emotion being triggered is GRIEF.

Now, I can EITHER rub the points that relate to grief and be done with it.

OR, if I'm unsure about how that all works and I want more clarity on what other patterns might be relevant to me I can start to work my way through a simple three-part matrix.

Step 1: Find Which Area of Life the Emotion Relates to

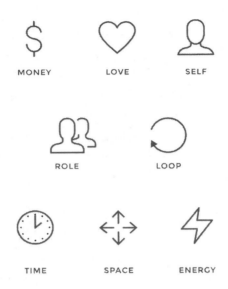

The first part of the grid can be thought of as three separate areas of life. Any emotion can loosely be categorized as relating to money, love or the self.

Money

Not enough money: – an unlock here indicates that the emotion is related to the loss of money, the belief that we won't have enough or the perception of being unworthy/not good enough or otherwise to the area of financial misfortune

Too much money: – an unlock here indicates that the emotion relates to something being too expensive or too much money is involved

Love

Romantic love: – relates to infatuation, erotic or sexual love, physical desire as well as passion

Family love: – relates to the love we have for our mother and father, tribal group, husband or wife, marriage and family or family-like organizations

Consciousness love: - the pure energy of unconditional love, cosmic intelligence or love that transcends human boundaries. Can also relate to intelligence

The Self

Self to self
- relates to any internal decision or conversation that takes place in our own head or perception we hold of ourselves

Self to other
- describes an energy, perception, action or intention that flows FROM us TO someone else

Other to self
- describes an energy, perception, action or intention that flows FROM someone else TO us

Self to situation
- the emotion relates to a situation or event rather than to another person, e.g. skydiving, public speaking or divorce. It isn't about the specific people involved but about the event itself

Step 2: Find the Structure of the Emotion

Once we know which area of our life the emotion relates to we can then find how it's structured. It's either:

A role:

Meaning that the emotion is triggered WHEN we are playing a specific role such as a father or mother, or a teacher or a human being, a bully or victim or any other 'character' we can think of.

The pattern is not active when we aren't playing this role. E.g. guilt relating to our role as a mother is not activated in situations that don't cause us to think of ourselves as a 'mother'

OR

A loop:

Loops are by far the more common way for an emotion to be structured. A loop means that the trigger activates an emotion which in turn causes us to feel a certain way (e.g. shame means we don't have enough energy) which then intensifies our shame because we have no energy.

Some loops will continue looping for YEARS on end until they are cleared!

Step 3: Find the Effect

Finally we have the effect of the emotion. Emotions warp our perception of reality by contracting or expanding our perception of time, space or energy.

Time:

This means the way we perceive the flow of events, our sense of urgency, relaxation, impatience or whether we believe something will ever actually happen

Too much time: I'll have to wait forever, it takes too long, it occupies too much of my time, etc.

Not enough time: we'll never make it, I can't find time for it, we're gonna be late, I never have enough time

Space:

This describes how much room to move we have (whether literally or figuratively) and how physically far away something feels

Not enough space: Claustrophobia, no room, self-disconnection, etc.

Too much space: Sense of overwhelm, something TAKES too much space or I feel too distant or miss someone or something

Energy:

The flow of vital force through our bodies and lives

Too much energy: It takes too much energy, it makes me hyperactive, overwhelming

Not enough energy: I'm drained, I can't put enough in, etc.

Step 4: Put it all Together

When we work our way through the grid we are able to narrow down what the emotional pattern is about, how it's structured and what its overall impact on our life is.

For example:

"I'm okay with losing my job"

This could map out as:
grief -$ loop +e
not enough money
loop
too much energy

Which would mean: "I feel a sense of loss, because I'm not going to have enough money coming in AGAIN and ... deep down it's going to cost me too much energy to find another one to get that money."

As we clear it the perception will change and we'll start to gain energy AND when we map the patterns and get familiar with them they start to tell us things about what we believe deep down.

For example, if I found that pattern it would tell me that I carry some beliefs about money being hard to come by and requiring too much energy. This would lead me to do some clears around wealth, such as the ones listed in the 'clearing maps' section of this book.

How Much Clearing is too Much?

Especially in the early days it's important to realize that there is a limit to how much clearing you should be doing. At first it can feel like you've found a magic wand, and in a way you have, but there's a price to pay for waving it at everything in sight!

When we clear an emotion it changes our perception. This means the physical body (including the brain and nervous system) has to 'catch up'. Our psychological maps of who we are and how the world works may need to shift around too.

This means, take it easy at first. If you do some clearing and then feel emotionally unstable in the following few days it's important to understand that's a part of the process (you aren't losing your mind) and to take care of yourself.

It's also important not to add to the burden by clearing a whole bunch more stuff straight away!

I think of it like Internet bandwidth. When I download a couple of movies at once they download quickly and smoothly. When I choose twenty different movies and try to download them all at the same time – the system can grind to a halt. The same thing applies to your mind/body and its processing ability.

If you find yourself having a tough time after clearing some emotions refer to the 'processing emotions' checklist in the reference section.

What if it's not Working/Unclear/ Nothing on the List Comes up?

If it's in the early days (say, your first three months of practice) you're going to have times where your focus is off and your self-trust isn't really built up yet.

The whole art of testing and clearing is based on INTENTION.

When we commit that "this will work" and "one of the emotions on the list will come up" then we train our intention to give us a clear result.

If you're getting mixed results, refresh your mind, move your body and come back to it with a curious but unattached attitude.

Often people that struggle initially are those who have a hard time trusting their instincts and listening to their intuition.

The question "What if I'm influencing the results?" may come up for you also.

Of course you are, you're talking to yourself; that's the whole point!

The key is to practice a lot until you don't think about it much. If you have a friend who is also learning clearing (you can find one in the study group) you can practice doing clears on each other. Clearing 'self-trust' and 'self-clearing' are a good place to start too.

All of the models and maps I've collated and created are just that – models. If you're going to use them take the attitude that "I want to know which of the words on this list is THE MOST ACCURATE" rather than "I'm not sure if any of these emotions are right". Your body WILL do what you train it to and the stronger your intention gets the more accurate and powerful your results will be.

If you REALLY aren't making progress, consider going through The Spiral and clearing up the shame/guilt/low self-esteem energies that are present in your life.

My promise to you is that if you practice this tool for at least twenty minutes a day for three weeks and just trust in it, you'll find you've hardwired the skill and you can then use it to create amazing change.

Integration Activities

The integration process is different for everyone and can depend on what you've cleared and how much you've cleared too.

Most of the experienced clearers I know have developed rituals and habits that speed up the processing of the emotions by the mind and body. These can include working out, having massage and chiropractic treatments, saunas, sleeping, drawing, journaling, etc. You can also muscle-test:

"What do I need to help integrate these clears?" and

"How long before the new behaviors are integrated?" to give yourself some support and clarity.

THE MENTAL
MODELS

Models are symbolic representations that help us to take a big-picture view of something. I've collected various models for understanding consciousness, manifestation, human evolution, the energetic body, etc.

My attitude once again is not so much that these are absolutely true; they're just frameworks that have helped me make sense of the world and that are particularly powerful when we combine them with clearing.

Here are some overviews of some of the most useful models I know of.

I give only a very simple introduction to these and suggest that you independently study the ones that you relate to or are inspired by. The purpose of me sharing these particular models is they can give you a context for what you are trying to achieve.

For example, the model of the five bodies helps me know the difference between whether the solution to a problem is to clear an emotion or to take some kind of physical action or to learn a new piece of information.

Many people get stuck in the paradigm they specialize in — for example, a surgeon will look for a surgical solution and a chemist will look for a chemical solution to a problem.

Not ALL things can be solved by clearing emotional blocks.

In addition to learning clearing skills I recommend developing good questioning skills to help you derive insight into what actions to take.

This is an especially powerful strategy when combined with muscle-testing and potent maps and models.

The Five Bodies

The beauty of the 'five bodies' framework is it gives us a chance to understand ourselves as multidimensional beings in a very simple way.

I often use this model to diagnose what LEVEL I should be working on to solve a specific problem or achieve a certain outcome. Many healing practitioners and people working on their own evolution lack a simple way of knowing which tools benefit which parts of ourselves. For example, no matter how many emotions I clear I'll never get bigger and stronger unless I eat right and work out in the appropriate way.

If I keep trying to clear more and more stuff around my physical body without taking measurable physical world action, I'm unlikely to really experience any measurable change in this area.

This may seem obvious but I hear it all the time.

People use meditation to try to change their belief systems. Or use Reiki to try to clear emotional patterns. Or do hypnosis to make more money. Or drink ayahuasca with the hope it will heal an emotional illness without ever actually considering:

"On what level is the situation I wish to change?"

"Which techniques and practices work most effectively on that level?"

Here is a List of the Five Bodies in Order of most to Least Dense:

1. The Physical Body

It's the one we see and deal with every day, the flesh-and-blood body comprised of bones, muscles, skin, lymphatic system, nerves, etc.

A physical manifestation would include things like a rash, a bruise, a broken arm, etc.

The physical body also relates to the realm of the manifest, including all physical objects like a house or a car or a table.

2. The Emotional Body

The emotional body is our FELT self. This is the level that clearing operates on most directly (although skillful and intentional application of clearing will include work on the other levels too).

This is the level on which we feel 'happy', 'sad', 'guilty' or 'afraid'.

The conditioning and complexes described in this book exist primarily on the emotional level (although they can have impacts on the other levels also).

3. The Energetic Body

This is the body of subtle (and not so subtle) energy flows. The meridian and chakra systems, the aura, chi gung, Reiki, etc. are all working on the energetic level.

Our energetic field and the flow of life force through our body can be thought of on this level.

4. The Mental Body

This is the realm of 'mind'. What we think, what we believe, our values, how we see ourselves in our 'mind's eye', etc. Processes like memorizing information, formulating mental stories, hypnosis, coaching, setting goals, thinking about things, primarily affect the mental body.

The mental maps and models you're taking on right now are creating change primarily on the mental level.

5. The Causal or Spiritual Body

This is the realm of 'soul' or of our infinite potential. We can't ever get harmed or damaged on the causal level. At this level we are complete and whole in every way.

Our connection to God/the universe is directly felt at this level. You could also call it our 'higher self'. Blocks in the other levels, however, can limit our ability to feel connected to this level.

How to apply this information?

Whenever you either identify a problem or set a goal ask yourself – on what level do I need to do work to handle that problem/create that outcome?

You can also muscle-test to see if there are any blockages or issues on other levels that affect the one you want to work on.

E.g. I keep stopping my diet because I have emotional patterns around body image that are interfering.

The most intelligent course of action would be to clear the patterns (emotional/mental) AND to go back to the diet (physical) with a renewed sense of clarity and confidence.

The Scale of Consciousness

POWER VS FORCE

	LEVEL	SCALE	EMOTION	PROCESS	LIFE-VIEW
	Enlightenment	700-1000	Ineffable	Pure Consciousness	Is
	Peace	600	Bliss	Illumination	Perfect
P	Joy	540	Serenity	Transfiguration	Complete
O	Love	500	Reverence	Revelation	Benign
W	Reason	400	Understanding	Abstraction	Meaningful
E	Acceptance	350	Forgiveness	Transcendence	Harmonious
R	Willingness	310	Optimism	Intention	Hopeful
	Neutral	250	Trust	Release	Satisfactory
	Courage	200	Affirmation	Empowerment	Feasible
	Pride	175	Dignity (Scorn)	Inflation	Demanding
F	Anger	150	Hate	Aggression	Antagonistic
O	Desire	125	Craving	Enslavement	Disappointing
R	Fear	100	Anxiety	Withdrawal	Frightening
C	Grief	75	Regret	Despondency	Tragic
E	Apathy	50	Despair	Abdication	Hopeless
	Guilt	30	Blame	Destruction	Condemnation (Evil)
	Shame	20	Humiliation	Elimination	Miserable

Power vs Force is one of the most influential books I've ever read. This scale created by Dr Hawkins has influenced the creation of all the tools you're now learning and become a major part of how I assess my own level of consciousness AND how I choose what I want to learn.

At the simplest level it's a measuring tool that introduces us to a vibrational take on how reality works. This vibrational worldview has been confirmed for me via numerous spiritual, psychedelic experiences and countless experiments with consciousness.

If we want to create a result of any kind we need to adjust our vibration to match that of the frequency we want to attract.

It just so happens that clearing (the right things) can help us rapidly adjust our vibration and change our state of consciousness.

The most effective way to use this tool is to start testing your own scale of consciousness and to experiment with the Energetic Field Clearing in the reference section of this book.

The Chakra System

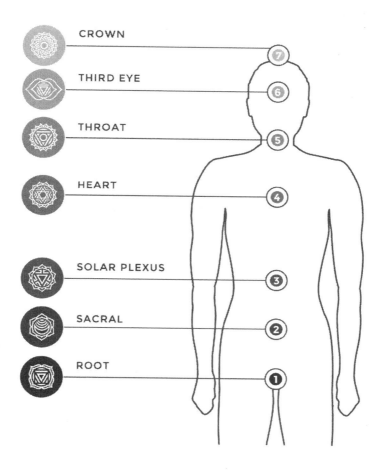

This is personally my favorite system for understanding reality. I love it because it applies to all levels (see the five bodies) and is anchored to our physical body.

Manifestation Clears use the downward flow of manifestation through the chakras. Chakra clearing uses the chakra model to clear resistance at specific levels. The Spiral process clears up a large amount of the baggage that prevents us developing the chakras.

Tantric Yoga has become one of my favorite life-enhancing practices. I work daily through postures that strengthen specific chakras depending on what I need more of in my life. I'll often muscle-test the strength and health of each chakra on a given day and tend to focus on cultivating a specific chakra for three to six months at a time.

The books *Wheels of Life* and *Eastern Body Western Mind* by Anodea Judith are two of the most popular and comprehensive books on chakras and I highly recommend them.

The 'Clear Your Shit' Emotions Chart

This chart can be downloaded from the Clear Your Shit website and many people have a copy on their digital device or have a copy printed out for when they do clearing work. The chart provides us with a way to language our unconscious experience and also shows us to a location on the body we can rub to shift the emotion.

I built this chart after about ten years of hybridizing three different Kinesiology charts and also pulling random emotions from various chakra books and books about emotion as well as from my own experience.

The power of this chart is that it creates a very broad palette to draw from whereas a lot of emotions charts are a bit shallow in their range. In the reference section of this book I've included an 'Emotions Dictionary' to give a simple definition for each one of the emotions listed (some appear twice in more than one meridian and have a subtly different flavor to them).

At a deeper level we can go really deep into the emotions and energetic structures that sit beneath our day-to-day experience. It's typical that as we do this work we go through stages. For the first few months of my clearing journey I cleared only Spleen and Kidney meridian emotions. My surface layers of stuff were all very Fear and Low Self-Esteem related.

Eventually I broke through those layers and anger issues began to appear. In this way I've journeyed through the majority of this chart and healed many past chapters of my life.

Another powerful exercise is that of root clearing emotions listed on the chart. If you want to do this, **please proceed with caution**. If you haven't done The Spiral, start with one root clear per day. If you have you can probably handle two or three at a time.

In this way you can root clear any emotion that relates to an area you want to be stronger in. For example, if you want to become more passionate and alive you could gradually work through the emotions in the FIRE element section of the chart.

It's not uncommon to experience the healing or disappearance of various symptoms of physical illnesses when we start working through emotions in this way. Disclaimer – this work CAN heal all kinds of physical illness IF the drivers of the illness are emotionally based. Although many illnesses do have an emotional component I advise against claiming you can heal physical symptoms with this work. Sometimes it happens but I view it as a side bonus because it's hard to guarantee when working with emotions exactly what the physical outcome will be.

The Buddhist Concept of Attachment

One of the central ideas of Buddhism is that attachment is the cause of suffering. In other words, events don't directly dictate our level of peace and contentment, our REACTIONS to those events do.

It's important to note that pleasure and pain will ALWAYS exist.

These are the polarities that make being human what it is.

Sometimes people express concern that using clearing will gradually dehumanize them. Over fifteen years my experience has been anything but that.

The more conditioning I've cleared, the more I've been able to feel a wide range of feelings and sensations, both pleasurable and painful.

These days, however, I SUFFER a lot less than I used to.

Life events will still happen and being human we will still have responses to those events. Emotion will flow through the body but because we RESIST it much less we are able to open to the richness and fullness of the emotion.

This leaves no residue behind.

If I perceive someone crosses my boundaries and I get angry, I am consciously aware of the anger, perhaps I take action, perhaps I don't, very quickly the anger passes and I am at peace again.

The use of clearing simply speeds up our ability to let go. That's it, really.

The ongoing, long-term use of this tool is compatible with various forms of Buddhist practice. I highly recommend finding a meditation practice that resonates with you to accompany this work.

I personally spend a little time each day practicing a slightly modified version of Vipassana meditation which helps me cultivate increased composure, calmness and acceptance (super helpful if you've cleared a lot of shit) as well as increased awareness of my bodily sensations and increased compassion and love.

Be – Do – Have

Of all the models I've learned from the personal development world, this is by far one of the most useful.

Most of the world confuses cause with effect.

We essentially see things as Have – Do – Be. "If only I had that athlete's body, then I could play sport like him and I'd BE a famous millionaire athlete."

In reality it works the other way round – the INNER BLUEPRINT of our being – our identity, our values, our beliefs and our energy impacts and drives our behavior – which in turn produces our results.

Because humans are VISUAL creatures we observe the results as though they are somehow the driving force when in reality they are a side effect of our inner blueprint and the actions we habitually take.

This is why modeling the behavior of others is only effective if we REALLY get what's going on inside their heads and then model the BEING as well as the DOING aspects.

Clearing when applied to the BEING level can help us create change at a deep identity level. When we step into a new identity, it's very easy to take action in alignment with it. If we continue taking action in the correct direction we WILL get the results.

What this means:

For us transformation enthusiasts this gives us a lot of power to create the results we want. When I do work on myself I'm usually looking for an identity to upgrade and a series of new actions and behaviors to implement along with it.

Over time I've found myself becoming much less attached to the outcomes I want (even though I still have a very clear idea of what it is I want to create) and spending a lot more energy on stepping into being the person I want to be and doing the work. If I'm not getting the results I want it's either on the BEING level or the DOING level or both.

This is present in the statements I use for clearing:

"I'm okay with BEING an athlete"
"I'm okay with BEING an entrepreneur"

The place I apply the BE/DO/HAVE model most regularly is in my life design process.

As I work through each of the areas of life, clarifying what it is I want to create, I make sure to address it at a BE/DO/HAVE level. For example:

Physical Health:

BE: a strong, healthy, athletic and attractive man
DO: weightlifting and strength training three times per week
HAVE: 90kg body with great muscle definition and able to deadlift 90kg by Xmas

Once we have this level of clarity for ALL the areas of our life we can then clear any resistance to each of the levels and work towards the outcomes we want with much less friction. In this way BE/DO/HAVE is an awesome model for creating what we want.

If you want further details on this, watch my 'Be/Do/Have' talk on the Clear Your Shit YouTube channel.

PART THREE:

TYPES OF CLEARING

The following section details the types of clears I've created and use regularly.

Although there are an infinite number of ways you can use this tool these structured clearing techniques are great for specific scenarios.

There are videos for all of these different styles of clearing on the Clear Your Shit YouTube channel.

Basic Statement Clearing

This is where everybody starts and during the course of everyday life I still use these simple clears constantly.

Never underestimate the power of just clearing the thing that's right in front of you. Although it's often not the heart of the issue clearing simple statements like:

"I'm okay with dropping out of college"

will often shift an emotion that lets you look at the situation more clearly.

The golden rule of clearing statements is:

ALWAYS CLEAR BOTH SIDES

For example, if you did clear "I'm okay with dropping out of college" you would also be clearing "I'm okay with NOT dropping out of college."

The reason for this is that attachment is attachment. The desire to push something away from us functions in exactly the same way as the desperation to bring something into our life; it keeps us emotionally attached which then causes us to have a confused perception about the issue.

So whether you want to be rich or not clearing:

"I'm okay with being rich" and
"I'm okay with not being rich"

are both necessary if you want to be able to be free to make clear decisions around money.

The basic way to test if you are clear with something is to form a statement about it in the form of:

"I'm okay with X"

where X is either a concept or a process.

For example:

"I'm okay with sex"
"I'm okay with money"
"I'm okay with religion"
"I'm okay with exercise"

If we want to work on a behavior (e.g. smoking) we can then start making statements that address the doing and the not doing of the behavior.

For example:

"I'm okay with smoking" and "I'm okay with not smoking"
"I'm okay with stealing" and "I'm okay with not stealing"
"I'm okay with exercising" and "I'm okay with not exercising"

We can also create statements that break down any part of the BE/DO/HAVE process.

"I'm okay with being a genius/not being a genius (be)"
"I'm okay with swearing/not swearing (do)"
"I'm okay with having friends/not having friends (have)"

If we want to get to the heart of the matter we would target BEING-type statements relating to the identity we want to clear:

"I'm okay with being a smoker/not being a smoker"
"I'm okay with being a fighter/not being a fighter"
"I'm okay with being an employee/not being an employee"

The number of statement clears you can find is limited only by your imagination.

On the subject of basic clearing you don't have to actually say anything or even use words. You can picture something in your mind's eye, FEEL a sensation in your body or even make a sound. We can clear ANYTHING that has an emotion anchored to it. Because we use language to understand our world, forming statements is one of the main ways to do it, but I'll often just imagine something and clear the image and feelings that go with it.

Body Clearing

Our body is the source of constant information in the form of sensations. It's also our vehicle for experiencing life on planet earth. Many of the pains, physical restrictions, sensations and tensions we feel on a daily basis are the result of emotions being stored in the body or contractions in the face of fears we are unconsciously harboring.

Many people I know clear headaches that disappear in seconds. I've also seen physical injuries (caused by accidents, etc.) heal quicker from clearing the emotions stored in that part of the body.

This is one of the most simple and intuitive forms of clearing but one that can change our level of health and also speed up our ability to learn new physical skills.

The simplest body clear I know is to just FEEL into an ache or pain or injury and ask:

"Are there any emotional issues present in this part of the body right now?"

If we get a "yes" we go ahead and clear it by working through the emotions chart as per usual.

A more in-depth form of body clearing is to feel into any area that has had repeated injuries or difficulties or even any area we are trying to rehabilitate or strengthen.

For example, during my morning workout, if I feel like my knees are stiff I'll pause for a few moments and start feeling into the specific muscles in the legs that connect to or surround the knee.

I'll test if each one has an emotion in it and if it does I'll clear it.

After doing this for one week I was able to squat all the way to the ground when previously I could barely make it halfway. Most of the emotions I'd cleared were 'fear' related which made sense to me as I was beginning to train my body to do things that were out of my old comfort zone.

Brain Clearing

Some mornings I wake up with an unclear head and can't concentrate or focus. Also when I'm working on one thing for a long time (like this book) I find my concentration fades and my head gets cloudy or distracted. Brain clearing can be helpful for this.

It's also useful when we're trying to learn something new and we keep 'switching off". Often there's an emotion behind the lack of focus.

It's amazingly simple.

Start by asking:

"Can I access my brain?"

You'll get a yes.

From there we journey through a few separate parts of the brain and measure what percentage they are running at emotionally.

The basic brain clears I do are:

Left brain: relates to logical process
Right brain: relates to creative or abstract process
Amygdala/lizard brain: relates to survival issues
Frontal lobe: relates to forward planning, goals, future vision, etc.

Corpus callosum: connects left and right brain hemispheres

I like to clear each of these sections to 100%. When you first start this you'll be amazed/disturbed by how many emotions are messing with your brain function.

Once all of these areas are clear you'll notice a DRAMAT-IC difference in the quality of your thinking/processing ability.

Clearing Complexes

You'll soon encounter situations in which clearing a simple statement doesn't seem to be enough. You'll clear the statement and you'll be able to feel there are more dimensions to it.

A 'complex' (for our purposes) is any package of ideas that group together, have an emotional charge attached and affect our behavior.

I like to make 'complex' clears that cover all levels of the BE/DO/HAVE formula in one go.

For example:

I'm okay with being a smoker/not being a smoker (the identity)
I'm okay with smoking/not smoking (the action)
I'm okay with having a healthy lifestyle/not having a healthy lifestyle (the result)

We can also find complexes around any concept:

Concept: confrontation
I'm okay with confrontation
I'm okay with BEING confrontational
I'm okay with not BEING confrontational
I'm okay with confronting my fears
I'm okay with not confronting my fears

Root Clearing

A root clear gives the ability to go DEEPER than the basic statements (although don't underestimate the power of clearing the RIGHT complex or the right identity when you're looking to change a behavior).

I created these in 2012 when I was finding that standard statement clears weren't getting to the CORE of the issues I wanted to deal with.

I'd been using the NLP timeline technique for a few years but I wasn't satisfied that:

a) it was really clearing the issues and that
a) most people's imagination were fine-tuned enough to access the information to the level required to do deep clearing work

I blended timeline with muscle-testing and started root clearing EMOTIONS. Big changes started happening. This simple process became the building block for the Spiral and I've watched root clears change people's lives in twenty seconds flat.

A root clear changes our whole relationship to something across our entire life. It does this by mapping WHEN we first attached various emotions to the thing that's triggering us.

We can apply a root clear to ANYTHING but they are most commonly applied to emotions (especially ones that keep coming up) and to key themes that are having an effect on our lives (e.g. money or confrontation or death).

Root clears follow a specific structure, meaning we are always looking for three separate time intervals in our life.

The first one: when we first formed an emotional response to the trigger

The second one: the second emotional response we layered over the top of the first one and

The third one: a summary of ALL OTHER residual emotions we have anchored to the trigger (also known as the 'residue')

How to do a Root Clear on 'Fear'

We are root clearing 'fear' which means we are clearing our relationship to fear.

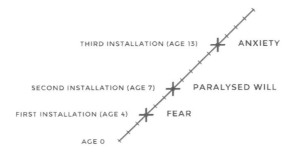

THIRD INSTALLATION (AGE 13) — ANXIETY

SECOND INSTALLATION (AGE 7) — PARALYSED WILL

FIRST INSTALLATION (AGE 4) — FEAR

AGE 0

1. We test to find the first age at which we anchored an emotion to FEAR and we find that at age four we anchored FEAR to FEAR. In other words, from four years old onwards we became afraid of fear itself!

2. We test to find the second emotion we anchored to FEAR; we find that at age seven we anchored paralyzed will to fear. This tells us that by seven we began to FREEZE whenever we were afraid and became incapable of action.

3. We find the third emotion at age 13 and find that it's ANXIETY. This final installation represents the 'residue' of all the other emotions that have occurred since the first two installations. In other words it's the last significant anchor we picked up in relation to FEAR. We've been living out our experience of FEAR based on the unresolved experience of our 4, 7 and 13-year-old selves over and over again!

Once all three installations (also known as anchors) are found, all you need to do is rub the points corresponding to one of them, breathe and release the pattern.

As always, we would check to see that we're done:

"Did I just successfully root clear fear?"

When we test a yes, we're done.

CAUTION:

Use root clears sparingly; they can be hard work for the body to process (you're essentially clearing three things at once) and doing more than two or three at a time can be VERY disorientating.

WHERE TO START:

If you're wanting to practice your root clearing but aren't sure what to start with you can start by working through any of the emotions on the Clear Your Shit emotions chart. Also, there are root clears (marked RC) for various purposes in the 'Clearing Maps' section of this book.

IF YOU DO A LOT OF THESE CLEARS IN A ROW YOU ARE GOING TO FEEL FUCKED UP.

The solution is to stop clearing for a few days, do some exercise, rest, cry, write in your journal, etc.

Chakra clearing is the exception to the 'stop clearing when you feel overwhelmed' rule. Clearing your chakras will typically help you re-stabilize and process the strong emotions unleashed by too much root clearing.

Quadrant Clearing

Quadrant clears are so called because they are a way of dividing any triggering situation into four separate, but interlinked possibilities.

Unlike most clears, quadrant are a great way to clear Limiting Beliefs and Complex Equivalences. They also aren't as heavy to process as root clears and can help you solve problems you don't understand just by working through a formula.

They look like this:

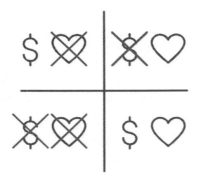

One of the things that happens to us as we grow up is we compartmentalize different areas of life and often adopt an either/or belief system.

For example:

I can either have money or be loved
I can either have freedom or commitment
I can either live my life purpose or have a career
I can either have a great sex life or meet a nice girl, etc.

Once again our emotions are shaping what we believe is possible.

If we grew up around parents who were always fighting it is reasonable to form the belief that it's an either/or between marriage and harmony or between love and happiness.

The statements that form the quadrant Love vs Money would sound like this:

I'm okay with having money and not having love
I'm okay with having love and not having money
I'm okay with not having love and not having money
I'm okay with having love and having money together

In other words the template is:

'Possibility A but not possibility B'
'Possibility B but not possibility A'
'Neither possibility A or B'
'Both possibility A and B together'

If you're unsure of where to start with quadrant clears the easiest thing to do is choose an area of your life you want to work on (wealth or love are great for quadrants).

Ask yourself WHY you want the things you want.

For what purpose do you really want money or a new lover?

What do you believe it will give you?

When you realize the real reason you want money is a value it represents to you like freedom or power or confidence then you can ask yourself:

"What do I believe it's going to cost me if I pursue that?"

We have many values conflicts, such as believing if we're wealthy we can't be honest or believing that if we fall in love we're going to lose our freedom.

Quadrants are great for clearing the blocks to realizing:

"I can have BOTH"

Make lists of things you don't think you can have at the same time like:

money and spirituality
love and freedom
success and friendship
power and compassion

Test up which examples you need to quadrant clear and away you go!

Wealth Clearing

Wealth clearing is anytime we use a financial measurement to track the effectiveness of our clearing.

The most common ones I use are monthly and yearly income measurements, but net worth, money in my pocket, savings, spending and numerous other metrics can be useful too.

With wealth clearing we are measuring the amount of money we are emotionally congruent with.

If I measure my monthly income at $5,000 per month that indicates that I'm emotionally congruent with $5,000 per month.

If I want to earn $20,000 per month I'm going to have a hard time emotionally pulling it off since it is four times what I believe I deserve.

Some of the clears listed in the 'money' section of the clearing maps will help to raise your wealth resonance.

Another way to do it is just to clear UP TO the amount you want to be okay with.

ADVICE – don't go too hardcore with this!

If you're stuck on $2,000 per month, try clearing up to $5,000 per month and keep it at that level for a month. You'll be amazed at what you're capable of during this time.

If we go back to the BE/DO/HAVE model, it's a no-brainer that if we genuinely want to make more money, we're going to have to take more action.

This could include making x amount of sale calls or taking an extra job or creating a new source of passive income. The money has to come from somewhere in the real world.

Having said that, after I do wealth clearing sessions with people who are already taking action (e.g. business owners and sales people) sometimes the most incredible opportunities fall straight into their laps. This is one area in which we can easily measure our results!

Using this method I went from $50,000 per year to $50,000 per month (in actual real money in the bank) over a period of eighteen months.

If you're serious about this, buy my book *The Conscious Hustle* or contact me via contact@danetomas.com for a wealth clearing session.

Chakra Clearing

Chakra clearing is one of the first things I figured out and I still use it on a daily basis as part of my morning practice. The main reason I do it is because it FEELS amazing – it creates a feeling of clear, open presence that lasts throughout the day and it makes it a LOT easier to get things done.

I'll also clear specific chakras when I'm doing activities that relate to them; for instance, root chakra before weight lifting, sacral chakra before sex, and throat chakra before public speaking.

The most basic level of chakra clearing is to feel into each chakra and ask the question "How clear is it?" on a scale of one to ten. Clear any emotions sitting in the chakra until it's a ten out of ten clear.

The next level of this process is to start seeing the chakra as a two-way energetic vortex. It both gives energy out into the world AND receives energy from our surroundings. We can clear each chakra up to ten out of ten for both giving AND receiving.

On top of this we can add the energy flow from the crown to the ground (the manifestation current) and from the ground to the crown (the liberation current).

These sixteen clears can eventually be done very quickly and can COMPLETELY change our state on many levels.

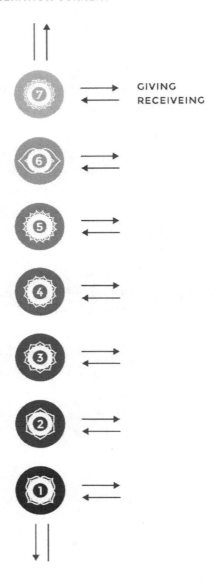

CHAKRA LINES:

As an extension to chakra clearing we can also clear the chakra LINES between ourselves and another person. This clear is useful when we can feel friction or contraction in our relationship with another person. To do it we simply feel into the connection between each of our chakras and the other person, testing as we go.

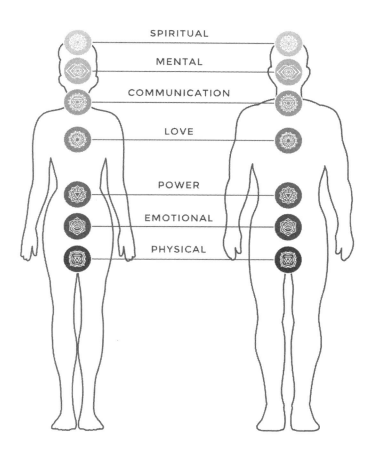

Manifestation Clearing

This is one of the most versatile clearing techniques. It utilizes the downwards current of the chakras to clear our ability to manifest an outcome. It can be used on a goal (e.g. building a house) or on a general life area (e.g. love and relationships).

To do a manifestation clear, we simply choose the goal or area we want to manifest success in and work DOWN through the chakras. It can help to understand the general theme of each one as it relates to manifestation. The areas that need clearing will relate to which level our manifestational current is blocked at.

For example.

7. Crown Chakra – alignment to purpose – why do you want it?
6. Third Eye – clarity of vision – what does it look like?
5. Throat Chakra – confident expression – how do you communicate it?
4. Heart Chakra – openness and organization – are you ready for it?
3. Solar Plexus – willpower – how much do you want it?
2. Sacral Chakra – emotional flow – how do you feel about it?
1. Root Chakra – action – what steps will you take?

As you clear you way down the chakras, holding the idea of what you want in mind you will gradually become clearer at each level.

For more on mastering this technique opt-in at clearyour-shit.com for the self-clearing videos (it's taught in lesson 5).

Manifestation clearing for business is also described in great detail in my book *The Conscious Hustle*.

Person Clearing

Clearing a person is great for improving our interpersonal relationships especially with people who seem to be able to push your buttons or people who you want to be able to co-create and cooperate with, such as romantic partner and business partners.

With this clear, what we're really doing is clearing up the emotions that were attached to WHAT THEY REPRE-SENT to us in our head. When it comes to dealing with other people this is where perception is projection REAL-LY kicks in.

The basic clears I do to clear up my relationship to a person are:

"I'm okay with (name)" (clears emotion attached to the idea of the person)

"I'm okay with (name)'s attitude" (clears emotion attached to how they think)

"I'm okay with (name)'s behavior" (clears emotion attached to what they do)

"I'm okay with (name)'s energy" (clears emotion attached to their presence)

"I'm okay with (name)'s values" (clears emotion attached to what they value)

"I'm okay with (name)'s world view" (clears emotion attached to how they see the world)

The person clear can then be joined with the chakra lines clear to shift the energies flowing between you.

This combination is later built on for when we learn quantum clearing.

Energy Field Clearing

In addition to clearing my chakras each morning, the other thing I do each morning is clear my energy field.

This was initially inspired by reading *Power vs Force* and thinking:

"Of course I could get my level of consciousness up to 1000!"

So I started clearing it each morning. As documented at the beginning of the book I became a clearer, less attached, more conscious and present human being. I also decided there were other dimensions to this clearing process and it gradually evolved to where it is now.

The three measurements that evolved were:

Consciousness – a vibrational measurement of how aware and how clear our capacity to perceive our experience is. Any low vibrational energies such as fear, guilt and shame will interfere with our ability to resonate at the highest level possible. From a tantric point of view this measurement relates to our masculine presence.

Buddha Field – how far out into the world do we allow our field to extend? Do we shrink our presence for fear of being judged?

Radiance – how BRIGHT will we let our light shine? Do we hold our spirit back? From a tantric point of view this clear relates to our feminine radiance.

1. Clear CONSCIOUSNESS up to 1000
2. Clear BUDDHA FIELD up to 10,000
3. Clear RADIANCE up to 100,000

Not everyone will find it easy to clear all the way up to the full measurements straight away and that's okay. I've found that people who have completed The Spiral have a much higher natural resonance than most people who haven't.

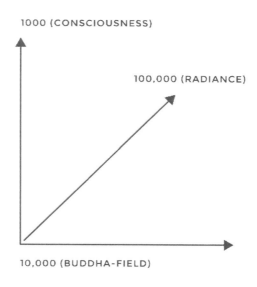

103

Archetype Clearing

Of the most powerful work I've done with masculine and feminine energies, working with archetypes has always played a part.

The word was introduced to us by Carl Jung and really describes an 'original type' or 'primal essence'. Archetypes can also be thought of as primal identities and are REALLY magickal when combined with clearing.

Commonly known archetypes would be the mother and the father. The major arcana of the tarot are all archetypes that can be worked with using clearing.

My Integrated Man men's program is based around a series of masculine archetypes aligned to the chakra system:

The Beast, The Lover, The Warrior, The King, The Poet, The Magician and The God.

These primal identities are powerful. They communicate vast amounts of information without needing to be described in words because they exist in our collective unconscious.

Working with archetypes is all about balance. I have spent some time working with 'The King' archetype, for example. Every now and then I'll muscle-test whether this archetype is in balance.

He represents order, justice, structure, organization, authority, wealth and a masculine nurturing capacity. In the book *King, Warrior, Magician, Lover* the archetypes are represented as triangles with an overactive side and an underactive side.

The overactive king is 'the tyrant', a bully who enforces his will on others, and the underactive king is 'the weak king', a man with no authority and integrity all due to his fearful, impotent nature. The 'balanced' king holds energy of fairness and measured power.

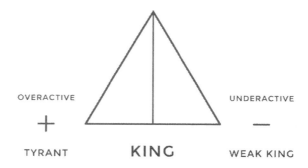

I use the following:
"I'm okay with being in my overactive king"
"I'm okay with being in my underactive king"
'I'm okay with being in my integrated king"

When all three are clear we are free to express the energy of the archetype in a balanced fashion. Combining archetype clears with ritual and practices that allow us to cultivate the qualities of the archetype is the best way to experience change and integration of archetype clearing work.

The Spiral

The single, most in-depth process I've created is The Spiral. Its purpose is to clear the largest amount of emotional baggage across all areas in the least amount of time possible. It's typically delivered over seven weeks (one session per week) but I have delivered it over a single weekend and have taken people through over the course of a year.

You should go through The Spiral process if you want to significantly raise your energetic vibration, if you want to leave behind a lifetime of accumulated baggage, if you want to accelerate your spiritual development and if you want to be a leader and influencer on a large scale.

The process can stir up some serious shit, but once the dust has settled the people that emerge have higher self-worth, vibrate at a much higher level, are more capable of attracting wealth and abundance and are more present and energetically attractive to be around.

If you're a crazy person (like me) and want to take yourself through the process, it's simply a matter of root clearing the following list of emotions (ideally three at a time).

What I recommend, however, is contacting me at www.clearyourshit.com and having one of the advanced clearing practitioners I've trained take you through this process. Not only are they experienced in this work and have taken many other people through, they understand the themes and challenges that take place as we move through each level and will be able to give you support and coaching as you take on one of the most life-changing processes on the planet at this time.

The Spiral Journey is a path through twenty-two emotions that are the emotions that most restrict our development as an integrated being. They are in order:

SHAME – a toxic and crippling sense of unworthiness
GUILT – a sense of failure to live up to a set of values or morals
DOGMA – rigid inability to see beyond our own prejudice

FEAR – a future-based projection of not being good enough
GRIEF – the inability to let go of the past
PARALYZED WILL – inability to act in the face of fear

PRIDE – attachment to the reinforcement of our own worth
ANGER – the impulse to react against the perceived violation of our boundaries
DESIRE – a sense of being pulled towards, of wanting

REASON – the ability to think clearly whilst remaining emotionally open

ACCEPTANCE – the ability to be okay with self, other and the present situation

LOVE – a sense of interconnected oneness and non-separate unity

ANXIETY – uncertainty of whether we can handle a future situation

CONFIDENCE – a sense of being 'good enough' that allows us to act

LOW SELF-ESTEEM – feelings caused by holding on to a negative self-image

TRUTH – being okay to see and accept the whole picture

TRUST – the ability to lean into life and let the universe take care of you

RECEPTIVITY – a sense of worthy, but vulnerable openness

PEACE – the appreciation of restful stillness and harmony

JOY – a vibrant aliveness permeating our being

ENLIGHTENMENT – the direct sense of our own infinite nature

PURPOSE – a divinely inspired sense of drive and meaning

Quantum Clearing

Inspired by Dr John Demartini's 'Breakthrough' process I designed the quantum clear in order to completely collapse the emotional projections around specific people in my life. Over time I used the process on everyone from my parents to world leaders, to Genghis Khan and Jesus Christ.

The power of the quantum clear is incredible. Every time we clear a person using it we recognize that there is nothing represented by that person that we don't embody in ourselves. In other words, when we run the quantum clear process on a world leader we systematically own our projections of that leader and will begin to embody the traits we see in them.

I'm not going to list specific instructions for quantum clearing here as

1. It's safe for people who've completed The Spiral only and
2. The process is complex and needs to be guided by someone who's done the full practitioner training with me

For those people who want to heal their relationship with their parents, let go of a deceased relative, heal the wounds of past abuse or let go of an ex partner completely – this process will do the job within a couple of hours.

If you want to be facilitated in a quantum clear by one of our practitioners you can book via clearyourshit.com

MAPS FOR CLEARING

One of the most common things I'm asked by those clearing at an intermediate level and beyond is:

"What should I clear to achieve x result?"

There are literally THOUSANDS of clears you can do but I decided to list some of the most important clears I use regularly in various areas of life.

Most of these will be "I'm okay with x" type statements and root clears. If you want to work on a specific area you can jump to that area and start clearing some of the concepts and behaviors named. As always, test to see if it's okay for you and to make sure you're not clearing too many things in one go.

Life Area: Social/Confidence

Statements:

I'm okay with …

listening/not listening

being exposed/not being exposed

being center of attention/not being center of attention

breaking the ice/not breaking the ice

making friends/not making friends

being inferior/not being inferior

being equal/not being equal

being superior/not superior

Root clears:

charm

confidence

extroversion

introversion

socializing

anxiety

inferiority

superiority

equality

Life Area: Money/Wealth

Statements:
I'm okay with ...
being narcissistic/not being narcissistic
being altruistic/not being altruistic
giving/not giving
taking/not taking
receiving/not receiving
allowing/not allowing
I'm okay with money as a means of exchange
being selfish/not being selfish
being evil/not being evil

Root clears:
money
worth
wealth
business
spending
saving
investing
value
finance
accounting
bookkeeping
tax
generosity
selfishness

Life Area: Business/Sales

Statements:
I'm okay with selling/not selling
I'm okay with marketing/not marketing
I'm okay with taking action/not taking action
I'm okay with being an entrepreneur/not being an entrepreneur
I'm okay with being an employee/not being an employee

Root clears:
business
sales
marketing
management
organization
entrepreneurship
vision
innovation
risk

Life Area: Creativity and Performance

Statements:
I'm okay with ...
being vulnerable/not being vulnerable
expressing myself/not expressing myself
being a creator/not being a creator

Root clears:
art
expression
stage fright
performance

Love and Relating

Statements:
I'm okay with loving myself/not loving myself
I'm okay with being caring/not being caring
I'm okay with being in love/not being in love
I'm okay with being abandoned/not being abandoned
I'm okay with being enmeshed/not being

Root clears:
love
romantic love
infatuation
devotion
compassion
intimacy
abandonment
enmeshment

Quadrant clears:
love v freedom
freedom v security
love v sex

Life Area: Sexuality

Statements:
I'm okay with ...
expressing my sexuality/not expressing my sexuality
connecting to my desire/not connecting to my desire
being a slut/not being a slut
being a prude/not being a prude
being sexually expressed/not being sexually expressed
being sexually repressed/not being sexually repressed

Root clears:
kissing
touching
foreplay
fucking
making love
having sex
transcendent sex
orgasm
annihilation
love
connection
transfiguration

Issue: Grief/Trauma/ Abuse

Statements:
I'm okay with …
being a victim/not being a victim
being a bully/not being a bully
being a rescuer/not being a rescuer
being an observer/not being and observer
respecting my boundaries/not respecting my boundaries

Tip:
Do a person clear on the specific abuser/bully

Root clears:
confrontation
boundaries

For someone who died/or you are separated from/you hate/you can't let go of:
"I'm okay with letting go of (name)"
'I'm okay with not letting go of (name)"
'I'm okay with hanging on to (name)"
"I'm okay with not hanging on to (name)"
"I'm okay with putting (name) in my heart"
'I'm okay with not putting (name) in my heart"
'I'm okay with forgiving (name)"
'I'm okay with not forgiving (name)"

Life Area: Spirituality

Statements:
I'm okay with …
being alone/not being alone
being attached/not being attached
letting go/not letting go
being present/not being present
being enlightened/not being enlightened

Root clears:
time
space
energy
enlightenment
death
meditation

REFERENCES:

1. SELF-COACHING & CLEARING FLOW CHART

This is a template that allows you to take yourself through a structured coaching and clearing process. It will allow you to set a goal, get rid of the blocks to that goal and then integrate the new behaviors you need to go and achieve it. All you need is a few sheets of paper and the ability to muscle-test answers to questions!

You don't need to know anything about what patterns you're running to find them using this process. You simply work through the steps answering the questions and when presented with options to choose from (e.g. in step three) all you need to do is to muscle-test which is the most accurate.

The steps in the process are:

1. Design your outcome
2. Make an honest assessment of where you are now
3. Find the obstacle
4. Clear it
5. Test to see if your done
6. Find an integration practice
7. Let go!

References:

Step One: Design Your Outcome

Answer the following:

What's your current goal or desire?
How do you want to feel about it?
What do you want to be capable of?
What will that look like?
How will you know when you've achieved that?

Step Two: Honest Assessment

Answer the following:

Where are you now?
What feelings are activated?
What do you perceive is in the way?
What are you afraid of?
What's the current situation costing you?

Step Three: Obstacles

What do you need to let go of to move forwards?
(Muscle-test to see which one is most accurate)

Is it a:

Story/Identity/Values Conflict/Belief/Action/Emotion/
Memory

Step Four: Clear it!

Which type of clear will be most effective?

Body Clear (scan your body and find the block)
Root Clear (of an emotion from the chart)
Statement (I'm ok with [insert challenge])
Quadrant (clash between two ideas/values e.g. Love and Money)
Person Clear (test up who specifically?)
Wealth Clear (how much do you need to be okay with?)
Manifestation Clear (clear the whole issue across all chakras)

Step Five: Test

Muscle-test the following?

Is that now clear?
Am I able to move towards my goal?
Is there anything else to clear? (if yes go back to step three)

Step Six: Integration

Which of the following activities will help me best integrate?

Muscle-test:

Visualization (picture the successful outcome)

Writing (three pages about what will happen now its cleared)

Physical (massage, sauna, sleep, exercise, chiropractic, other)

Action (take a single, simple step towards your goal)

Step Seven: Let Go

What's the best way to change state?

TV/sex/sleep/food/exercise/book

2. MIRROR THEORY QUESTIONS

So there's something pissing you off and you don't want to admit that it's got anything to do with you. Or maybe you can feel it but you have no idea how to language it.

Here are the basic questions I ask myself:

What does that person/event represent to me?
What is the key trait he/she has?
What type of character is he/she?
What feeling is this making me feel that I don't want to?
What area of inadequacy in me is this exposing?
If I wanted to call the person a name what would I call them?
What is the one thing about this I CAN'T accept?

Go through the answers to those questions, find the most triggering thing you've found and turn it around on yourself. Ideally you should end up with a statement like:

"I'm okay with being a fraud/not being a fraud"
"I'm okay with having integrity/not having integrity"

Or unpleasant concepts like:

"betrayal"
"selfishness"
"persecution"

You'll know when you're on the right track because the word you come up with will feel disgusting. The more we suppress the concept or behavior, the stronger it will feel.

When the trigger is an event or something you're sabotaging ask yourself:

"If I had that thing – what would it give me?"
and then "and what would THAT give me"
and then "and what would THAT give me?"

Eventually you'll chunk up from:

going to the gym
to having a hot body
to being attractive
to being loved!

The REAL issue is "I'm okay with being loved/not being"

3. PROCESSING EMOTIONS

Clearing your shit doesn't just make it disappear. Anything that's been suppressed has to be felt to be released. Sometimes this is easy and other times it's hard and uncomfortable.

Below is a simple step-by-step process that will retrain the way you deal with emotions that come up and make the journey easier and gentler.

1. Connect with your Body and go into the Emotion

All emotions take place IN the body. Oftentimes we don't even KNOW what it is we're feeling.

The first step is to stop doing what you're doing, breathe deeply into the belly and FEEL what's actually going on. Stay with the feeling and gradually allow yourself to sink into it deeply.

I guarantee there's a lot more stuff moving around in there than you realize.

What does it FEEL like? Can you stay present to it?

Is it heavy? Light? Open? Contracted? Painful? Pleasant? Warm? Cool?

References:

Get used to connecting into yourself regularly, learn to BE with the FEELINGS and do your best to fully experience what's going on without resistance or trying to 'push it away'.

2. Identify the Emotion

How would you describe it? Our emotional vocabulary determines how subtly we can actually FEEL. Keeping track of what emotions you have cleared recently REAL-LY helps. Is this what 'guilt' feels like for you? If you feel 'anger' ask yourself, "Is it really anger?" What else is in there? Do you feel 'hurt' or 'grief' beneath it?

If so – about what or towards whom?

Notice the dialogue that's going on. Most emotions will have accompanying stories, words or sounds.

For (stuck) emotions to be created in the first place there MUST be some sort of story or identification or attachment to SOMETHING going on.

If you listen closely and feel into yourself you might just hear or sense what's being said!

3. Love and Appreciate the Source of the Emotion

Don't get me wrong – I don't necessarily 'like' it when unpleasant, suppressed emotions come up to the surface either. Sometimes it feels terrible!

129

The key is though – we should NEVER make the emotion 'wrong'.

This does nothing to reduce the intensity of it and just sets the cycle of suppression in motion once again.

Every time an old emotion comes up – it's best to think of it as a young and confused part of yourself.

If a scared three-year-old turned up you probably wouldn't tell them to "Shut the fuck up" and "Get over it" and you wouldn't push them away.

You would find a way to soothe them and let them know that you loved them and appreciated them. Dealing with emotional patterns is no different.

The best thing we can do is FEEL down deeply into the source of the emotion and send an intention of love or "It's okay" or even intend a smile into it.

Most of our patterns were created long ago (many between the age of zero and seven).

Somewhere amongst the many layers, a young and vulnerable part of you is running a program that's designed to keep you 'safe'. Connect into that part as profoundly as you can (closing your eyes and placing your hands on your body can help) and really let it know that "everything is okay", that "you are loved" and that it's okay to "let go" of the emotion if it's ready.

4. Ask Questions/Use Self-Testing to Gain Insights

Once the wounded part of us has been soothed we can begin to gather some of the learning from the emotional process that's taking place. There are messages and insights coming up from the unconscious in the form of feelings and sensations – what are they?

There are many great questions we can ask in reference to what's going on, such as:
"What is this emotion trying to tell me?"
"What is it trying to keep me safe from?"
"Do I need to change something in my life?"
"Is the emotion still needed?"
"What else would I like to feel right now?"
"If I knew I was whole and complete would it be okay to let go of it?"

In terms of self-testing it's a game of narrowing it down using yes/no questions.

"Does it relate to THIS area of my life? This one? This one?"
"Does it relate to THIS person? This one? This one?"
"Is it about my past?"
"Is it about my future?" etc.

5. Feel Yourself Handling it in the Now

When things feel overwhelming the first question I ask myself is: "Is this going to kill me?" Usually the answer is no!

I like to go through all the different outcomes in my mind and feel into whether I could handle them or not. Not will they "feel good" but ultimately "Will I be okay?" or "Will I come out the other side of this?"

The eventual answer is always yes. We DO have all the resources we need but sometimes we have to go through and see and feel all the different possibilities before we can become certain of that.

Ask yourself – "What will it look like when I come out the other side?"

Now you can connect into the present. Breathe and bring your concentration into your breath. Does this emotion exist in the present or is it dependent on you running a memory or projecting a story of what might happen in the future? When we are completely present in this moment we are in a space of love, gratitude and openness. A place of 'there just is'.

References:

6. See Yourself Handling it in the Future

Once you're getting present and the emotion is gradually reducing in intensity the best thing to do is realize YOU CAN HANDLE IT. In fact, you've probably overcome this emotion in the past too. Now set the clear intention that you will be able to easily overcome this emotion in the future. Imagine yourself fully feeling the emotion in the future and letting it subside. See yourself acting despite the emotion and neither suppressing nor being overwhelmed by it. Build strong certainty that when emotions come up you simply open through them, love yourself and let them go.

7. Take a Specific Action

The Spiral and self-clearing work show the body how to let go of emotions and the steps above will help you to process them.

The next thing to do is to take an action that demonstrates to you that you are ACTUALLY changing.

After all – that's the reason you're doing this work in the first place – to get some different results.

What is the simple, immediate action you could take RIGHT NOW that would signify an increase in your mastery of this emotion or behavior?

133

Sometimes it's as simple as making a phone call, tidying the house, attending a dance class or having a conversation with someone.

Once you step into new territory you will BEGIN TO REALIZE ALL THE WAYS IN WHICH YOU ARE CHANGING. If you NEVER do anything new you may have changed emotionally but never actually notice!

Clearing is akin to taking off the emotional handbrakes: until you accelerate your vehicle forwards you don't get to find out how much easier it is to move forwards.

Once you see yourself speaking, moving, acting, thinking in a new way you will begin to realize FOR REAL you are leaving your old patterns behind and stepping into a new, empowered, integrated, truer version of you!

4. EMOTIONS DICTIONARY

FIRE ELEMENT
Emotions in this element relate to our fire:
aliveness, arousal, creativity, passion, wildness, etc.

SMALL INTESTINE (SI) (how we feel deep inside)
vulnerability – a deep sense of being exposed and unprotected

joy – a vibrantly alive sense of peace

shock – an abrupt sense of surprise and upset

unappreciated – the feeling that others do not value us

hurting – an ongoing sense of emotional injury

sadness – poignant sense of loss

sorrow – abiding feeling of distress caused by loss

nourishing – the ability to absorb love and sustenance

nervousness – overactive and unstable

discouraged – loss of desire to move forwards

internalization – the choice to head inwards rather than feel pain

overexcited – excessive elation or hyperactivity

assimilation – the process of being absorbed into

HEART (H) (the center of our being)
love – beautiful sense of oneness, unity and connection

joy – a vibrantly alive sense of peace

hate – the burning refusal to love

pride – an egoic self-assessment of being good

self-confidence – sense of capability

self-esteem – healthy and resilient self-image

self-worth – knowing that one is good enough

135

self-doubt – being unsure of our capability or values
caring – a sense of concern for others
acceptance – allowing what is to be what is
forgiveness – letting go of perceived harm in the past
compassion – unconditional desire to love others
anger – fiery reaction to having our values or boundaries challenged
security – feeling of being safe and protected

TRIPLE WARMER (TW) (resistance to challenge)
hope – a sense of reassurance based on faith in a future outcome
resilience – ability to withstand any circumstance or condition
lightness – a radiant, uplifting quality
muddled instability – a sense of unsettling confusion
service – a humble energy of helpfulness
balance – a sense of homeostasis
buoyancy – a sense of uplifted spirits
invulnerability – inability to feel pain or be harmed

CIRCULATION SEX (CX) (sex, fertility, creativity)
lust – strong, all-consuming physical desire
creativity – the state of fulfilling innovation and birth
receptivity – openness to take into oneself
stubbornness – resistance to change
arousal – rising sense of energy and aliveness
renounce the past – to let go of a specific event or story
responsibility – the burden of taking care of others
depression – the suppression of energy
desire – a sense of wanting that pulls us towards
generosity – to be overflowing with the desire to give

References:

tranquility – a delicious sense of peaceful calm
hysteria – uncontrollable outburst of emotion

EARTH
Emotions in this element relate to groundedness, heaviness, nourishment and stability

SPLEEN (SP) (energy, self-worth)
low self-esteem (LSE) – abiding negative self-image
confidence – the belief in oneself and one's abilities
sympathy – feeling of resonance with
empathy – taking on feelings of others
brooding – to dwell heavily in the same depressive state
cynicism – fear-based negation of positivity
rejection – to feel cast out and pushed away
envy – to hate someone for what they have
consideration – to pause and reflect before acting
recollection – to go back into a past event
indifference – numbness and disconnection from outcome

STOMACH (ST) (absorption, breaking things down)
empathy – taking on feelings of others
sympathy – feeling of resonance with
disgust – strong desire to reject and push away
worry – recurring concern about future outcomes
criticism – to pick apart and reduce the value of
unreliable – not to be depended on
disappointment – sadness at having one's expectations go unfulfilled
fulfilment – the sense of having everything we want
hunger – the desire to be filled
nausea – a sense of sickness and unease

greed – addictive need for MORE
harmony – a beautiful sense of equilibrium and peace
doubt – nagging uncertainty
emptiness – a sense of nothingness

METAL
Emotions in this element relate to cutting ties, letting go and heaviness

LUNG (L) (release, vital force, expansion/ contraction)
grief – the suffering caused by not letting go of the past
guilt – a form of self-judgment caused by not living up to a rule or standard
regret – looking back on the past and wishing it could have been different
letting go – the act of releasing past events
depression – heavy emptiness caused by suppressing one's feelings
openness – transparent sharing of one's truth
cheerfulness – an air of upbeat joviality
humility – to be down to earth and unpretentious
prejudice – holding a biased view without engaging with the truth
contempt – to be disgusted by something or someone

LARGE INTESTINE (LI) (letting go, depth, deep unconscious)
dogma – uncompromisingly rigid thinking
guilt – a form of self-judgment caused by not living up to a rule or standard

References:

shame – a deep sense of unworthiness and disconnection from the tribe

spite – the directing of hurtful energy outwards in an attempt to harm

vulnerability – a sense of not being guarded

release – the sense of freedom that accompanies letting go or being let go of

self-worth – recognition of one's own value

letting go – the act of releasing

hanging on – the act of clinging onto

reason – clarity of mind

depression – heavy emptiness caused by suppressing one's feelings

sadness – poignant sense of loss

mercy – the choice to not inflict harm or pain

WATER
Emotions in this element relate to flow, creativity, instability, change and the unconscious mind

BLADDER (BL) (pressure and release)

pissed off – passive aggressive and bitchy expression of anger

paralyzed will – inability to take action

terror – strong fear of being annihilated by something larger than ourselves

horror – an intense feeling of fear, shock, and disgust

anxiety – uncertainty of what's to come

inadequacy – a sense of not being good enough or capable enough

impatience – the sense that events are taking too long to occur irritation – a sense of recurring discomfort and slight anger

fear – the projection into the future of pain, suffering or loss

frustration – the belief that you can't get what you want

dread – the certainty that something bad is about to happen

KIDNEY (K) (power/powerlessness)

fear – the projection into the future of pain, suffering or loss

dread – the certainty that something bad is about to happen

anxiety – uncertainty of what's to come

phobia – a one-off fear of a specific event (always an image)

sexual insecurity – fear that one isn't good enough sexually

creative insecurity – fear that one isn't good enough creatively

superstition – drawing irrational, fear-based conclusions

paranoia – irrational fear of a specific future event (image)

caution – the attempt to control events in order to avoid fear

disloyalty – fear of betrayal/betraying

carelessness – disconnection of heart in order to avoid fear

bad memory – a specific unpleasant past memory causing fear

WOOD
emotions in this element relate to growth and expansion

GALL BLADDER (GB) (venom and disillusionment)

resentment – anger at perceived self-sacrifice or loss

impotence – utter powerlessness (including sexual)

repression – forceful withholding of urges and desires
self-righteousness – to assume moral superiority
bitterness – to be continually pissed off by past emotional hurt
forbearance – ability to endure unpleasant conditions
boredom – lack of joy in current events
helplessness – to be powerless to change a situation
humility – forced inferiority
choice – regret and anger around a specific decision

LIVER (L) (reactivity and change)
anger – reactive desire to force change to occur
rage – violent anger
fury – wild hysterical expression of passion and anger
frustration – irritation caused by not getting what we want
transformation – the feeling of dramatic and total change
distress – destabilizing sense of overwhelm
vengefulness – strong desire to wreak harm
hostility – open enmity for others
discontent – dissatisfaction caused by comparing reality to an ideal
jealousy – hating someone else because they have what you want

CENTRAL MERIDIAN (feminine side/body)
shame (often sexual shame) – unworthiness or dirtiness related to the body
self-respect – seeing oneself as worthy of admiration
confidence – sense of being worthy and capable
shyness – a feeling of social awkwardness
self-consciousness – to be overly concerned of how one is perceived

peace – a sense of restful stillness

overwhelm – the sense that everything is too much

embarrassment – to be ashamed about how one is perceived

vulnerability – being exposed and unprotected

support – the sense of being held up and taken care of

GOVERNING MERIDIAN (masculine side/spirit)

integrity – a sense of alignment between one's divine and human selves

purpose – a sense of drive connected to one's spiritual mission

truth – recognition of the fullness of what IS

trust – the sense that everything will be okay

harmony – tranquil equilibrium

humiliation – forced degradation and fall from grace

false pride – pretending to be proud to avoid vulnerability

arrogance – the forced persona of being above or superior

enlightenment – to be beyond the material world

response-ability – ability to respond

success – creation of a positive outcome

References:

5. INTEGRATION ACTIVITIES

When a pattern is cleared it may begin to shift immediately but new behavioral patterns, beliefs, identities and other adjustments will take time to integrate. There can also be a physical delay as the body makes rebalances itself.

It can be wise to ask questions after a big clearing session:

How long will this take to integrate?

Do I need to do anything to support the physical integration?

Do I need to do anything to support the non-physical integration?

Test the following list for inspiration.

Physical integration strategies:

extra rest: e.g. naps, early nights, sleeping in
light exercise: e.g. walking, swimming, social dance, tai chi
strong exercise: e.g. kickboxing, weight training,
rock-climbing
physical therapy: e.g. massage, chiropractic, Reiki, acu-
puncture, sauna
nutrition: taking vitamin or mineral supplements, fresh
organic food, hearty meals

Non-physical integration:

The following activities can assist with releasing old stories and opening to new ones:

journaling: write for twenty minutes per day for three days in a row

ritual: create a ritual to release what's been cleared/bring in something new

practice: go and do the EXACT thing you cleared – e.g. make sales calls if you cleared rejection, self-pleasure or have sex if you cleared 'arousal'

life redesign: using the life redesign forms on the CYS website, redesign your life vision

References:

6. GLOSSARY

Anchor – an emotional response associated to a trigger

Attitude – a specific way of thinking or feeling about something

Attachment – the inability to let go of something

Belief – a feeling of certainty about what is or isn't true

Baggage – the emotional accumulations that weigh us down

Conditioning – the process of acquiring habitual responses

Clearing – the process of severing the link between a trigger and response

Collapse – to bring opposing elements together in a way that nullifies the emotional charge

Chakra – an energetic center that connects us to the world around us

Consciousness – the phenomena that allows us to perceive and have experience

Complex – a package of associated ideas or beliefs that have an automatic emotional response attached to them

Emotion – an energy with a specific-feeling flavor that moves through the body

Emotional block – an emotion that is locked in a repetitive pattern

Filter – the perceptual veils we observe the world through that determine what we do and don't take in from our surroundings

Integrate – to become more whole and cohesive

Loop – an emotional pattern that re-triggers itself over and over

Mirror theory — a framework of ideas supporting the philosophy that the external world can be understood as a reflection of the contents of our mind

Meridian — energetic pathway as described by Traditional Chinese Medicine

Projection — attributing our own repressed thoughts and emotions to another person, institution or event

Pattern — a behavioral structure that keeps recurring

Role — a specific persona or identity

Shifting — the physical sensation of feeling emotional patterns leaving the body

Trigger — the event that causes the emotional reaction to take place

Value — ideal or standard that we consciously or unconsciously deem to be important

7. FREQUENTLY ASKED QUESTIONS

1. I try to muscle-test but I don't trust it?

   This is normal. The rule of thumb (pun intended) is PRACTICE MORE. Clear lots of things. Don't worry about whether you're doing it right. Practice every day for three weeks to a month. Try clearing 'self-clearing' and 'trusting myself/not' also.

2. Why do the same emotions keep coming up over and over again?

   Our conditioning tends to pile up in layers just like layers of rock build-up over time. Over a period of time we'll chip away at certain kinds of patterns and behaviors to eventually break through to the next level. As certain issues clear (I cleared poverty stuff for a couple of years!) new ones will come to the surface. If you're getting impatient consider booking in for The Spiral. You can also root clear the emotions that keep recurring.

3. How do I know what actions to take to integrate what I've cleared?

   Generally you need to devise activities that will force you to expand past what you've cleared. For example, if you cleared 'being shy' go and join a public speaking group for a few months. If you cleared 'investing' start learning share trading. Once we've changed on the BEING level it's important to try out some new actions!

4. How can I stop from taking on other people's stuff?

    If you're a healer or just particularly empathic clearing your chakras and the lines between you and other people regularly is imperative. Taking on other people's baggage is called 'surrogating'.

    Over time you'll clean up your own energetic field and you'll become less susceptible to other people's 'stuff'. Doing the energetic field clears and raising your vibration higher will serve to immunize you against low frequency emotions to a degree.

5. I've cleared my own patterns relating to other people and it seems like they've changed?

    This is where it gets weird. When we change our perceptions of others do we also change the others? It's impossible to know for sure but it seems so. I've witnessed people that hated me warm to me and become supporters when I cleared blocks around them. I've also seen massive changes happen in family members as we clear ancestral stuff that's been passed down for generations.

6. Since I've started clearing I've had more arguments with my partner than before – what's happening?

When we're in an intimate relationship we inevitably form energetic patterns and loops between our partner and us. There are all sorts of ways in which we subtly manipulate each other to get attention, security, intimacy, etc. As we clear up our own stuff and become more self-loving this can actually make us an uncomfortable mirror for our partner.

They may unconsciously feel rejected or hurt as we change certain aspects of ourselves and stop 'playing along' with some of the old habits that we were so comfortable with previously.

This can cause short-term upset but if we have a good connection with our partner we will both gradually adjust over time and find new ways to get our needs met.

8. FURTHER READING

MIND, BODY, EMOTIONS
Power Versus Force – Dr David Hawkins
Verbal Questioning Skills for Kinesiologists – Jane Thurnell-Read
The Body is the Barometer of the Soul – Annette Noontil
You can Heal Your Life – Louise Hay
The Brain That Changes Itself – Norman Doidge MD
Touch for Health – Dr John Thie
The Biology of Belief – Bruce Lipton
The Presence Process – Michael Brown

PERSONAL DEVELOPMENT AND PSYCHOLOGY
Get the Life you Want – Richard Bandler
King, Warrior, Magician, Lover – Robert L. Moore
The Winner's Bible – Dr Kerry Spackman
The Breakthrough Experience – Dr John Demartini
The Conscious Hustle – Dane Tomas
Spiral Dynamics – Don Beck
Psychomagic – Alejandro Jodorowsky
Awaken the Giant Within – Anthony Robbins

SPIRITUALITY AND PHILOSOPHY
Wheels of Life – Anodea Judith
Eastern Body, Western Mind – Anodea Judith
Tantra – Osho
Tantric Transformation - Osho
Am I Going Mad? – Marlyse Carroll
What the Buddha Taught – Walpola Rahula
The Integral Vision – Ken Wilbur

9. PROGRAMS

Self-Clearing FREE Video Training

This free seven-part video program was designed to accompany this book and will give you the basic foundations you need to take clearing into your everyday life.

It also gives you access to our growing clearing community via a private Facebook group where you can ask questions that are answered by me and a handful of my senior practitioners directly.

Enroll at:
www.clearyourshit.com

The Spiral
The ultimate emotional baggage-clearing program is now available worldwide. If you feel you're ready to bulldoze your way through a lifetime of conditioning and emotional baggage and set your real self free to live a more authentic, higher vibrational existence on this planet – get in touch with us via the thespiral.com website. Not everyone is accepted into The Spiral program so an application process has to be followed to determine who's ready for this potent work.

Advanced Clearing Practitioner Training
If you really resonate with this work, Dane runs annual practitioner training intensives with small groups of dedicated individuals. The people who attend these courses are

usually practitioners of various other disciplines or people who have experience with powerful shifts as a result of applying clearing to their own lives. The training gives a deep immersion into the techniques as well as an energetic initiation into the heart of what clearing is all about. Enquire directly at:

contact@danetomas.com

Integrated Man – Masculinity Coaching

Dane Tomas also works directly with men around presence, purpose and sexual potency. For those wanting to read more of Dane's writing and for men wanting to attend one of Dane's workshops or work with Dane one-on-one – applications can be made via the www.danetomas.com website or Dane can be contacted directly at contact@danetomas.com

ABOUT THE AUTHOR

Dane Tomas is a writer, personal transformation innovator and creative entrepreneur.

He is passionate about many aspects of life, although key themes in his work include consciousness expansion, masculinity, entrepreneurship, awakened sexuality and self-expression.

To contact Dane for writing, talks, workshops, coaching or performances:
send a message to contact@danetomas.com
to learn more about Dane go to www.danetomas.com

NOTES

NOTES

NOTES

NOTES

NOTES

NOTES

NOTES